THE
INFORMATION SOCIETY

COMMUNICATION

A series of volumes edited by:
Dolf Zillmann and **Jennings Bryant**

THE
INFORMATION SOCIETY
ECONOMIC, SOCIAL, AND
STRUCTURAL ISSUES

EDITED BY
JERRY L. SALVAGGIO
Corpus Christi, Texas
Whataburger, Inc.

LEA LAWRENCE ERLBAUM ASSOCIATES, PUBLISHERS
1989 Hillsdale, New Jersey   Hove and London

For Lorraine

Lawrence Erlbaum Associates, Inc., Publishers
365 Broadway
Hillsdale, New Jersey 07642

Library of Congress Cataloging-in-Publication Data

The information society: economic, social, and structural issues /
    edited by Jerry L. Salvaggio.
        p.   cm.
        Bibliography: p.
        Includes indexes.
        ISBN 0-8058-0103-0
        1. Information technology—Economic aspects.   2. Information
    technology—Social aspects.   I. Salvaggio, Jerry Lee.
    HC79.I55I536   1989
    338.4'700151—dc19   88–24472
                                                                    CIP

Printed in the United States of America
10 9 8 7 6 5 4 3 2 1

Contents

Preface

This book's origin can be traced back to *Telecommunications: Issues and Choices for Society,* a book that I edited in 1983. At the time, the mass media was extolling the merits of information technology with the result that scholars turned to the consequences. My book was a reflection of that concern.

Scholars are still studying the social impact of technology. However, a new body of literature has evolved since 1983, which is sufficiently different from earlier scholarly concerns to warrant another book. The emphasis of the new approach is less on the consequences of information technology than on understanding the nature of information societies.

The inspiration for the new focus lies in the work of Daniel Bell, a Harvard sociologist who is perhaps more responsible than any other single scholar for the new perspective. Bell revealed the importance of information technology and its role in transforming industrial societies. His original essay, published in the aforementioned book, sought to understand what it is that makes an information society different. That essay is reprinted in this book.

There is still much concern over social problems. Invasion of privacy, computer crime, control of information, information inequity, and unemployment due to automation continue to be studied as their existence is no longer a matter of speculation. The study of information societies, however, has matured as is evidenced by essays in this book— many of which are written by young scholars.

The new position has raised a new set of questions. How does the infrastructure of an information society differ from that of an industrial society? Both Benjamin Bates and Jorge Schement review the literature in this area and examine some of the structural differences. How will individuals work and live in information societies? Judith Larson and Everett Rogers have studied Silicon Valley as a microcosm of information societies. The result of their study offers a glimpse of how individual life patterns might change as society moves from industrialization to information-oriented communities. What is the definition of an information society? Charles Steinfield and I review the literature on this subject and attempt to delineate some of the major characteristics of information societies.

William Dutton examines how different societies have attempted to pave the way for technology by developing wired cities. Herbert Schiller's essay reflects his continuing concern with government's involvement in information technology. His essay makes a cogent point and provides ample examples of military funding of information systems.

I would like to thank all of the authors for agreeing to allow me to include their essays in this volume.

1 Toward a Definition of the Information Society

CHARLES STEINFIELD
Michigan State University

JERRY L. SALVAGGIO
Corpus Christi, Texas

INTRODUCTION

It has become commonplace to allude to the United States, Japan, and several Western European nations as information societies. In much of the popular press, as well as scholarly journals, authors readily use the term information society with little or no operational definition. The expression is now so hackneyed that the Japanese have taken to designating Japan as an "advanced" information society. Despite this de facto classification by those writing about related topics, a review of the literature explicitly concerned with emerging forms of social organization reveals considerable debate over the precise nature of the information society. Although most concede that Western industrialized nations and Japan have experienced dramatic social, economic, and technological changes, there is little consensus on the nature and direction of the change. Yet, without an adequate conception of the nature of an information society, attempts to project social problems in information societies is difficult. In this chapter, we attempt to synthesize the varied work on information societies, and extract from the literature a set of core characteristics on which there appears to be some scholarly agreement. In so doing, problems with existing conceptualizations are raised, dissenting views are noted where possible, and the need for empirical research to more objectively define, measure, and test predictions about proposed societal transformations is noted.

1

Virtually all scholars agree that information itself has taken on a greater importance in highly industrialized societies. Many were influenced by the seminal work of Price (1963), who distinguished between information and knowledge and demonstrated the exponential growth rate in the production of scientific knowledge. From a beginning of two scientific journals in the mid-17th century, the number rose to about ten journals by the year 1750, 100 by 1800, 1000 by 1850, and an estimated 50,000 in 1963. Bell used the growth of books in university library holdings to illustrate a similar exponential growth pattern of information.

Other authors look at the pervasiveness of information in other areas. Porat (1977) focused on the information content of an increasing proportion of occupations, whereas the Japanese studies examined the sheer amount of information available to households. Huber (1984) looked at the information environment of organizations in the information society, concluding that the amount available is large and increasing.

Economic Base

A related, but slightly more controversial research perspective that reappears with some consistency places an emphasis on the importance of the information sector to the economy of an information society. Machlup (1962), Bell (1973), and Porat (1977) all focused on various aspects of the growing information sector in the United States. Komatsuzaki (1986) demonstrated a growing information sector in Japan, and Schement, Lievrouw, & Dordick (1983) observed the growth of information occupations in California. Not all agree with this perspective. Gershuny (1978) took issue with Bell's starting point of the growth of the service economy. He developed the concept of the "self-service" economy, where households invest in large consumer durable goods and computers in order to provide their own services. Information technology in this conception is merely another form of physical goods to be bought and sold. It has been depicted as international in scope (Dizard, 1984; Masuda, 1981). However, this concept of the information society points to the problem of unemployment created by the new international division of labor (Bjorn-Andersen, Earl, Holst, & Mumford, 1982; Mosco, 1982; Smythe, 1985). In spite of the debate, however, the locus of most of the above studies is the economy of the information society.

Technological Infrastructure

Another universal attribute of information societies is the influential role of information technology. Although not necessarily viewed as a causal factor, information technology nevertheless interacts in critical ways with economic, social, and political structures to produce social benefits as well as problems. Most authors point to the rapid innovation in computer and telecommunication technologies and their increasing availability across all segments of society (Salvaggio, 1983).

RESEARCH PERSPECTIVES

Although many schemes are possible, we classify the literature on information societies into five broad groups according to the attribute or sets of attributes emphasized by the authors. In a sense, each group represents a unique perspective. The five perspectives which we have identified include: a) economic structure, b) the consumption of information, c) technological infrastructure, d) critical approaches, and e) multidimensional approaches. In the following sections, we briefly review representative work from each perspective category.

Economic Structure

Nearly all who write about information societies point to the growth of the service sector in the industrialized nations and the decline of employment in manufacturing (Bell, 1973). For a number of authors, however, the dominant characteristic of an information society is the nature of its economy. Machlup (1962) initiated this research perspective by analyzing the growth of the "knowledge sector" in the U.S. economy. In Machlup's analysis, industries primarily concerned with the production and distribution of knowledge (hence, "knowledge industries") were examined separately, rather than as a part of the overall service sector. The knowledge industries included such areas as the educational system, the media and other communication activities, libraries and other information activities, and research institutes. The contribution of this sector to the gross national product was found to be significant (estimated at about 40% for the early 1960s) and growing at a rate considerably higher than the industrial sector. Machlup concluded that knowledge industries would soon outpace the industrial sector, leading to the rise of a "knowledge society." A similar conclusion was reached at about the same time in Japan, as Umaseo (1963) predicted the rise of the "spiritual industries" over material and agricultural sectors in economies that were more evolved. Essentially, Umaseo's spiritual industries, based on a biological metaphor, served the planning and control functions of society. Hence all activities concerned with the production and consumption of information were included.

These earlier approaches distinguished the knowledge or information sector from other economic sectors. More recently, the overall occupational structure of the economy has come to be associated with the transition to an information society. Porat (1977) initiated much of this work, by broadening the view of information work to apply to more than those jobs falling within the information or knowledge sector as defined by Machlup. Porat began by defining information activities as including all resources consumed in producing, processing, and distributing information goods and services. He defined the primary information sector as including all those businesses involved in the exchange of information goods and services in the marketplace. In addition, however, Porat noted that a great many jobs in other sectors of the economy can be thought of as information work. Nearly every organization produces, processes, and distributes information for its own internal consumption. Thus, a secondary information sector includes these information activities. Porat estimated that overall information activities accounted for 45% of the gross national product in 1967, and that half of the labor force was employed in information-related work. This study, perhaps more than any other, has been used to justify references to the United States as an information society. Moreover, several recent papers have attempted to refine Porat's analysis and apply it in other contexts (e.g. Komatsuzaki, 1986; Schement, Lievrouw, & Dordick, 1983).

A research perspective that places its focus on the information economy as the primary attribute of the information society has both conceptual appeal and empirical support. Examining the economic structure alone, however, provides only a limited view of the social and cultural implications associated with information societies. Moreover, the concepts and methods employed by these researchers has received substantial criticism. Several critics contend that Porat's classification of information workers is far too broad to be meaningful, and does little to suggest social implications of the shift to an information society (Bates, 1985; Dizard, 1984). Bates, for example, noted that according to Porat, factory workers assembling information transmission equipment are considered information workers, just as are university researchers. He felt that such broad categorizations weaken the social distinctiveness of the information sector, and such a unidimensional view of information societies says little about their evolving social functions, structures, and values.

Consumption of Information

A second research perspective on information societies is concerned with the consumption of information goods and services rather than their production (Bowes, 1981). This research, conducted almost exclusively in Japan, has come to be known in Japanese as *johoka* ("Informationalization") shakai ("society") research (Ito, 1980). Based on the work of Machlup and Umaseo, the Japanese initiated a series of studies attempting to measure the degree of *johoka* in Japanese society. Two studies by the Research Institute for Telecommunications and Economics (RITE) in 1968 and 1970 (cited in Ito, 1980) developed a methodology for measuring the degree of johoka based on two indices. First, the *joho keisu*, or information ratio was defined as the ratio of household expenditures for various information-related activities to total household expenditures. (Unfortunately, Ito noted that this was operationalized by subtracting *non*information expenditures from total expenditures to arrive at the amount spent on information activities.) The second component, known as the johoka index, was a complex measure made up of the following three categories of data as well as the information ratio (Ito, 1980; p. 16):

A. Amount of Information
   1. Telephone calls per person per year
   2. Newspaper circulation per 100 people
   3. Books published per 1,000 people
   4. Population density (a measure of interpersonal communication)
B. Distribution of Communication Media
   1. Telephone receivers per 100 people
   2. Radio sets per 100 people
   3. Television sets per 100 households
C. Quality of Information Activities
   1. Proportion of service workers in total labor population
   2. Proportion of students in total appropriate age group

Thus, while retaining an element of the economic structure approaches, these studies were primarily concerned with behavioral measures of consumption of information goods and services. In fact, the later study (RITE, 1970) attempted to formulate a very precise definition of the post-industrial, or information society, concluding that such a society should have the following characteristics.

1. A per capita income of more than $4,000.
2. The number of service workers exceeds 50% of the total labor force.

3. University students exceed 50% of the total appropriate aged population

4. The information ratio is greater than 35%

The information-consumption research tradition in Japan has continued, primarily with a series of yearly studies conducted by the Ministry of Posts and Telecommunications, the government ministry that funds RITE (MPT, summarized in Ito, 1980; 1984). These studies attempted to measure the total amount of information flow in Japan, became known as the annual "information flow census." Further differentiating this research tradition from those focusing on economic structure, MPT researchers examined the amount of information consumed by the Japanese people each year, with consumption interpreted as the *perception* of information rather than the *purchase* of information. One goal of this research was to measure the difference between the supply of information and the amount consumed. A methodology was developed and enabled researchers to convert all media—personal, mass, and performance—into a common unit, the word, for comparison. Thus, tables for converting radio, still pictures, moving pictures, and so forth into word units were developed based upon some rather controversial assumptions. Over time, these studies were used to demonstrate growth in the use of personal electronic media, a leveling off in the consumption of broadcast media, and a decline in the consumption of nonelectronic media. Moreover, the amount of information consumed was shown to be shrinking relative to the amount available, leading some to feel that the Japanese were suffering from information overload. These types of findings were used to rationalize the development of information policies in Japan that stressed the development of high capacity, interactive computer and telecommunication networks over traditional broadcast and nonelectronic communication systems.

The johoka shakai research perspective encourages us to look beyond the occupational structure, and incorporate the communication and information behaviors of people into our definitions of information societies. Moreover, the attempts to develop a standardized measure that can be applied across different societies are noteworthy. Attempts have been made, for example, to apply the information flow census to the United States (Pool, 1982; 1983). However, the actual measures used are crude at best and provide little insight into social and political structures and values that may be associated with information societies.

Technological Infrastructure

Among the more common orientations to the information society are those that focus on diffusion of computer and telecommunications technologies as the defining characteristic. Although information technologies occupy a central role in all of the information society literature, this research perspective emphasizes the technological infrastructure almost to the exclusion of other social, economic, and political attributes. Indeed, this literature is generally futuristic in perspective and invariably optimistic about the impacts of technology. Martin (1977; 1981; 1984) provided a number of scenarios detailing life in the information, or wired society. In particular, the spread of digital networks was viewed by Martin as the key element in the wired society, affording all a higher quality of life. The greater productivity such technology enables, for example, was viewed as reducing the amount of time we all need to work, resulting in increased leisure time. The specter of increased unemployment and economic hardship is not a part of this vision of the information society. Likewise, Smith (1971) felt that tremendous social advantages would follow the implementation of national broadband cable networks forming a "wired nation."

On a more realistic level, Dizard (1984) was sensitive to the social, economic, and political realities surrounding the diffusion of computer and communication technologies. However, he also viewed the information society primarily in terms of the spread of "communications networks and information machines." Information societies come about, according to Dizard, in three stages. First, the technological infrastructure is created by both large firms and small innovative companies. Then, all segments of the economy and government become dependent on information technology and communications networks. In the final stage, the mass consumerization of information technologies and services affords all a lifetime access to information.

Nora and Minc (1980), in an influential report to the French government, also recognized the moderating effect of political and cultural tradition on technological implementation. They are grouped with this section, however, because their analysis predicates the dramatic social, economic, and political change in France upon emerging telematics technologies (i.e., the convergence of computer and communication technologies). Telematics was seen by these authors as increasing productivity, but causing short term unemployment. It further will foster decentralization of administrative structures and promote the competitiveness of small and midsize businesses, thereby moderating power relationships. Moreover, the social status of technical professions will increase, as will overall contact between social groups. Finally, threats to sovereignty are anticipated as multinational corporations like IBM encroach upon the power of the state by controlling telematics networks.

On the other hand, Nora and Minc noted that in contrast to these likely outcomes of the widespread implementation of telematics, French traditions "favor centralization and administrative proliferation, hierarchy rigidity in big business, and the domination of small business by big business" (Nora & Minc, p. 6). Like Dizard, their view, then, is not really deterministic, as they called for the creation of a deliberate policy vis-a-vis telematics, arguing that the technology can only "facilitate the coming of a new society, but it cannot construct it on its own initiative" (Nora & Minc, p. 6).

The technological infrastructure perspective effectively draws attention to the potential benefits of information technologies for society. However, with such weighty emphasis on technology generally removed from a social, cultural, and political context, it, too, is unable to provide an adequate foundation for defining the attributes of information societies. Moreover, unlike the economic and consumption approaches, this perspective is not characterized by empirical research, making it difficult to objectively compare across different societies or measure any one country's progress toward becoming an information society.

Critical Approaches

A fourth perspective takes issue specifically with those who foresee social benefits resulting from the large scale introduction of information technologies. These authors recognize that technologies are a political and cultural product, and argue that its implementation and use will serve the interests of those in power. Information societies, according to this group, are best characterized by the omnipotence of large and powerful corporations who can best afford the high cost of the technology (Salvaggio, 1983; Schiller, 1981; Mosco, 1983; Smythe, 1985). Smythe (1985) in fact, viewed discussions of the information society as rhetoric designed to promote the sale of information hardware and software. He provided the historical context for inequities in the United States and argues that information technology will be used primarily to "redistribute income so that the poor get poorer and the rich richer (Smythe, 1985; p. 14). The information society in the view of these authors is one characterized by economic and information inequities, unemployment among the masses, deskilling of jobs to weaken the power of workers, and domination of governments by large, multinational organizations. Moreover, new information services directed to home markets will be new vehicles for advertising, continuing the ex-

ploitation of home consumers as commodities to be bought and sold
by the business community (Mosco, 1982; Smythe, 1978). Other scholars
in this perspective have called attention to particular social problems,
such as invasion of privacy, information control and computer crime.
The critical theorists have helped to focus our attention on the influence of the existing socio-political order in moderating any effects
of new information technologies. For the most part, however, these approaches remain as much captives of the value systems of the authors
as the "blue sky" literature. Little room for any social benefits of information technology is left, and, like the literature in the previous section, the lack of empirical research limits objective comparisons.

Multidimensional Approaches

Perhaps the most influential work describing the nature of information societies is that of Daniel Bell (1973; 1979), although he rejected
the term "information society" as being too limiting, and preferred
"postindustrial society" instead. Bell's conception is explicitly
multidimensional, as he defined a set of relevant dimensions along
which the various stages of societies may be compared. He traced the
evolution of societies across three stages—preindustrial, industrial, and
postindustrial—by analyzing their differences along the chosen
dimensions.

Changes in the economic sector are dominant among Bell's dimensions. In particular, postindustrial society is characterized by a service
economy rather than a goods-producing economy. Bell (1979) noted that
in 1970, 65 out of every 100 persons in the labor force were engaged
in service activities. Most important among the service occupations in
the postindustrial society are the human services, such as health, education, and social services, and professional occupations represented by
scientific and technical activities. Moreover, although rejecting the name
information society, Bell saw information and knowledge as key resources in the postindustrial society, in much the same way that labor
and capital are central resources of industrial societies. Following from
this, just as the transportation and energy infrastructures are critical
in preindustrial and industrial societies, the communications infrastructure, and in particular, computers and networks, are transforming
resources in the postindustrial economy.

Bell's postindustrial society is a decidedly rational place. The rise of
modern science and technology has led to the codification of theoretical
knowledge. Advances in this society are dependent upon this body of
theory, making significant training and education a prerequisite for success. Moreover, the complexities of postindustrial society are managed

by applying what Bell called a new "intellectual technology," characterized by systems analysis and decision science techniques that substitute
algorithms for intuitive judgments. He speculated that there is the
possibility of the formation of a new elite, comprised of scientists and
members of professional/technical occupations. At one point, he sur-
mised that this is not necessarily an unfortunate development, as these
types of people are more likely to be rational and egalitarian.

Masuda (1981; 1982) developed a similar multidimensional framework
to compare the technology, socio-economic structure, and values of an
information society with an industrial society. In contrast to the rational
image portrayed by Bell, however, Masuda presented a more utopian
model of the information society. According to Masuda's model, for example, the economy of information societies will no longer be based
upon such principles as the division of labor and the separation of production of goods and services from their consumption. Rather he proposed that there will be a "synergetic" economy, with information the
primary commodity produced and jointly used by both information
utilities and the users. He foresaw a better planned society, where goals
maximizing the common good of society rather than the principle of
supply and demand are used to order society. Moreover, in place of
the enterprise as the most important arena for social activity, Masuda
substituted voluntary communities oriented toward the "principle of
synergy and social benefit." Other value-laden phrases permeating
Masuda's topology of the information society include political rule by
participatory democracy rather than parliamentary democracy, social
change by citizens' movements, and the replacement of materialistic
values by goal achievement values.

It is better to think of Masuda's framework for the information society
not as a general definition of all information societies, but as an "ideal
type." His is a model of the social possibilities, rather than a realistic
assessment of the attributes of information societies.

At least one other scholar has considered the multidimensional framework of an information society. Bates (1984) extracted a set of dimensions
from the literature that serves to differentiate information societies from
earlier stages of societal development. Like Masuda and Bell, Bates organized attributes into economic, social/structural, and cultural/value
groupings. Bates, however, focused on the degree of consensus among
conceptions of information societies. He argued that multidimensional
approaches are necessary, as one dimensional approaches provide little
insight into the overall social framework of an information society.

Bates also suggested that there may be more than one type of information society. Bates even questions whether there is or will be an information society that is distinct from the industrial society. He questioned, for example, whether computer and telecommunication networks

are simply another form of physical capital, the dominant attribute of an industrial society. In support of this line of reasoning is the recent revelation that most successful information services have been financial services marketed to businesses, rather than the consumer-oriented videotex systems forecasted for information societies (The information business, 1986). The commodity, then, is either information hardware (i.e., physical capital) or information about money (i.e., financial capital) rather than information as a unique economic good. Bates concluded that rigorous social science research and theory is needed to help define the information society, particularly if we wish to direct the development along more desirable lines.

We have provided a review of attempts to define the nature of information societies. First, we caution against views of the information society that arise from a strict, technologically deterministic perspective. Most conceptions of the various stages of society have at their roots elements of technological determinism. Thus, transitions from hunting-gathering to agricultural, industrial, and finally information societies are generally viewed as occurring because of technological developments. In this most recent stage, the spread of computers and telecommunications networks are credited with ushering in a new pattern of social organization. An alternative approach, however, is to view technological developments as arising out of a particular society and culture. In essence, technologies are a cultural and ideological product rather than the reverse (Salvaggio, 1983; Slack, 1986). Using this perspective, we can then account for diversity among the various nations that are considered to be information societies, as each has a distinctive ideology and culture influencing the development, implementation, and use of information technologies. Salvaggio (1983) proposed that distinct national ideologies shape the way in which technology is used. Thus computer networks may be used for social control in one society and for business transactions in another. The utility of this model is that it explains why similar technologies do not have similar consequences in different societies.

A second, related point is that information societies are not solely defined by the technological infrastructure in place, but rather are multidimensional phenomena. Bates (1984) pointed out that any information society is a complex web consisting not only of a technological infrastructure, but also an economic structure, a pattern of social relations, organizational patterns, and perhaps other facets of social organization.

Finally, Huber (1984) warned against developing conceptions of information societies that are totally based upon extrapolations from recent trends. He noted that any system that is supposedly in a transition phase will undoubtedly engage in exploratory behavior in order to cope with environmental changes. Given this assumption, it is unlikely that recent trends would be strong predictors of the eventual attributes of information societies that have stabilized. It becomes important, then, to examine long term trends rather than recent history.

NEW DIRECTIONS FOR RESEARCH

From the above review it can be seen that although scholars agree that we are becoming an information society, there is little consensus on what it is that is inherent in information societies. Still, throughout the many diverse research perspectives some dimensions seem to reappear. The degree of emphasis given to these dimensions, the context in which they are used, and the values given them may differ. It is likely that no single perspective from which to view information societies can ever accurately represent the many manifestations to be found among the advanced industrialized nations of the world. Rather, many unique information societies are likely to evolve due to the complex interaction of the various dimensions that exist.

In addition to the attributes of information societies reviewed earlier, several other characteristics merit further attention. These include 1) the pervasiveness of information and the relationship between information and knowledge, 2) temporal characteristics, and 3) spatial characteristics.

Information societies are characterized by intensive knowledge bases, coupled with efforts to convert information into knowledge. The more information generated by a society the greater the need for turning this information into knowledge. Bell and Machlup have emphasized this dimension in their pioneering studies. Decision sciences, computer models and future studies are just a few of the methods that have evolved in information societies in an attempt to convert information to knowledge.

Another new dimension of information societies relates to the speed at which information is generated and distributed. Financial transactions in one part of the world are recorded in London, New York, and Tokyo in seconds. Computer conferences, videoconferencing, and electronic mail has virtually eliminated time lags in communication. This temporal dimension of information societies has yet to be studied.

Information activities seem not to be as dependent on transportation and large metropolitan centers in the way that industrial activities were. This has led to the re-emergence of a spatial dimension characterized by decentralization. Small, innovative organizations located in areas such as Silicon Valley or Austin, Texas, are now vying with large urban centers as a consequence of the power and utility of information.

In addition to the various perspectives examined in the first part of this essay and the three dimensions discussed above, many other attributes may be significant in shaping modern information societies. Additional research needs to be conducted on the claims made by scholars representing each of these perspectives. Meanwhile, new dimensions of the information society are now just unfolding.

ACKNOWLEDGMENT

Charles Steinfield is grateful to the Ameritech Foundation for their generous support of his research activities during the preparation of this chapter.

REFERENCES

Bates, B. J. (May, 1984). *Conceptualizing the information society: The search for a definition of social attributes.* Paper presented to the International Communication Association, San Francisco.

Bell, D. (1973). *The coming of post-industrial society.* New York: Basic Books.

Bell, D. (1979). The social framework of the information society. In Dertouzos, M., & Moses, J., (Eds.), *The computer age: A twenty-year view* (pp. 163–211). Cambridge, MA: MIT Press.

Bjorn-Andersen, N., Earl, M., Holst, O., & Mumford, E. (1982). *Information society: For richer, for poorer.* Amsterdam: North-Holland Publishing Co.

Dizard, W. P. (1984). *The coming information age.* New York: Longman.

Gershuny, J. (1978). *After industrial society: The emerging self-service economy.* Atlantic Highlands, NJ: Humanities Press.

Huber, G. P. (1984). The nature and design of post-industrial organizations. *Management Science, 30* (8), 928–951.

The information business. (1986, August 25). *Business Week,* pp. 82–90.

Ito, Y. (1980). The 'Johoka Shakai' approach to the study of communication in Japan. *Keio Communication Review, 1,* March, 13–40.

Ito, Y., & Ogawa, K. (1984). Recent trends in Johoka Shakai and Johoka policy studies. *Keio Communication Review, 5,* March, 15–28.

Komatsuzaki, S. (1986). An economic impact of informationization. *Keio Communication Review, 7,* March, 13–24.

Machlup, F. (1962). *The production and distribution of knowledge in the United States.* Princeton, NJ: Princeton University Press.

Martin, J. (1977). *Future developments in telecommunications.* Englewood Cliffs, NJ: Prentice-Hall.

Martin, J. (1981). *The wired society.* Englewood Cliffs, NJ: Prentice-Hall.

Martin, J. (1984). *Viewdata and the information society.* Englewood Cliffs, NJ: Prentice-Hall.

Masuda, Y. (1981). *The information society as post-industrial society.* Bethesda, MD: World Future Society.

Masuda, Y. (1982). Vision of the global information society. In L. Bannon, U. Barry, & O. Holst, (Eds.), *Information technology: Impact on the way of life.* Dublin: Tycooly International Publishing.

Mosco, V. (1982). *Pushbutton fantasies: Critical perspectives on videotex and information technology.* Norwood, NJ: Ablex.

Nora, S., & Minc, N. (1980). *The computerization of society.* Cambridge, MA: MIT Press.

Pool, Ithiel de Sola. (1982, January). *Communications flows in the United States: A census, with comparisons to Japan.* Research Program on Communications Policy. Massachusetts Institute of Technology.

Pool, Ithiel de Sola. (1983, August 12). Tracking the flow of information. *Science,* 221, 609–613.

Porat, M. U. (1977). *The information society.* Washington, DC: US Department of Commerce.

Price, D. de Solla. (1963). *Little science, big science.* New York: Columbia University Press.

RITE (Research Institute of Telecommunications and Economics). (1970). The roles of telecommunications in a post-industrial society. Tokyo.

Salvaggio, J. (1983). The social problems of information societies. *Telecommunications Policy,* 7 (3), 228–242.

Schement, J., Lievrouw, L., & Dordick, H. S. (1983). The information society in California: Social factors influencing its emergence. *Telecommunications Policy,* 7 (1), 64–72.

Schiller, H. (1981). *Who knows: Information in the age of the fortune 500.* Norwood, NJ: Ablex.

Slack, J. (1984). *Communication technologies and society: Conceptions of causality and the politics of technological intervention.* Norwood, NJ: Ablex.

Smith, R. L. (1971). *The wired nation.* New York: Harper and Row.

Smythe, D. (1978). Blindspots about western marxism: Reply to Graham Murdock. *Canadian Journal of Social and Political Theory,* Spring-Summer, 109–127.

Smythe, D. (1985, April). *An historical perspective on equity: National policy on public and private sectors in the U.S.A.* Paper presented to the Thirteenth Annual Telecommunications Policy Research Conference, Airlie House, VA.

Umaseo, T. (1963). On information industries. *Hoso Asahi,* January, 4–17.

2 Evolving to an Information Society: Issues and Problems

BENJAMIN J. BATES
Michigan State University

Society is not static. It is, in the terminology of general systems theory, an open system: A dynamic set of interrelated social systems, institutions, and individuals that act upon and react to various aspects of the world around it. Open systems exist in a state of constant flux, continually reacting and adjusting to changing conditions and developments from both within and without the system. Generally, these changes and adjustments are evolutionary—small changes and modifications in a system's structures, interrelationships, or patterns of behavior that better permit social systems to survive in a climate of changing conditions. Occasionally, however, factors or influences may arise whose impact is truly revolutionary, forcing a more abrupt and drastic modification in the social system, resulting in a wholesale transformation in social institutions and relationships.

Scholars, scientists, and philosophers have been predicting such a revolutionary transformation of modern industrial society almost since the Industrial Revolution was accepted as an example of revolutionary social transformation (Machlup, 1962; Ellul, 1964; McLuhan, 1964; Brzezinski, 1970; Bell, 1973; Lamberton, 1974; Porat, 1977; Boorstein, 1978; Dizard, 1982). There have been hundreds of predictions and discussions about the implications of such a revolutionary transition, in what probably amounts to thousands of articles, across many disciplines. Despite the popularity of such concerns about the next stage of societal evolution, there has been little consensus as to the causes and results of that proposed social revolution. Hence, there are almost as many

15

labels for the resulting new society as there have been treatments.[1] Although there have been just about as many causes identified as transformations, most treatments concur in finding one driving force behind such major social transformations as being the result of, or related to, rapid development and diffusion of information technologies.

Although most scholars have predicted that the rapid expansion of information technologies and activities will at some point radically transform societies in which it occurs, others have argued that such a social revolution is now in progress or has already occurred. That is, some researchers have stated that some countries are, in fact, already "Information Societies," and that other societies are actively seeking to facilitate and promote that transformation. Marc Porat (1977, 1978) has been among the leaders in proclaiming the United States as among the first of the "Information Societies" (also Parker, 1981). Japan has also been held to be well on its way toward the establishment of an information society (Bowes, 1981; Masuda, 1981; Salvaggio, 1983). The vision of the "Information Society" as the society of the future also seems to be generally accepted throughout Western Europe, where many states have developed policy for encouraging the transformation (Benedetti, 1980; Nora & Minc, 1980; Bowes, Sullivan, & Wheeler, 1985; Snow, 1985). Similar efforts have been undertaken in Canada (Ganley, 1981), Brazil (Branco, 1982), Australia (Karunaratne, 1984; Cullen, 1985), and elsewhere in the Far East (Jussawalla & Cheah, 1983; Langdale, 1984), as both developed and developing countries seek to take fullest advantage of the perceived benefits of the Information Revolution.

The classification of any society as having undergone such a radical social transformation, however, is still somewhat suspect; the evidence presented in such cases argues more for the existence of an Information Economy than an Information Society. Such considerations usually are based on the reclassification of aggregated national economic data on the size of an identified information sector, rather than the identification and observation of any revolutionary social transformation. Most thinking on the Information Society has remained on the abstract, theoretical level, focusing on the identification of current trends and extrapolating their likely (or potential) consequences. And even then it has been suggested (Bates, 1984) that the trends and factors identified as the basis for revolutionary impact may themselves be only evolutionary extensions of the fundamental guiding forces of Industrial Society rather than the harbinger of a revolutionary social transformation and the coming of a new age.

At this point, the question of whether information and information technology are outcomes of the growth-oriented, economic (some

---

[1]James Benigner (1986) recently listed over 70 separate "transformations" identified since 1950.

would say capitalistic) forces of the Industrial Society or whether they are the basis for a revolutionary social transformation remains unclear. This issue is clouded by inconsistencies among the definitions and basic concepts utilized by scholars and the inherent problems of observing and measuring the various aspects of information in the form of goods and services, which are said to be at the heart of the Information Revolution. What seems to be certain, although still not clearly observed or measured, is that information and information technologies are assuming a more central and important role in modern society. However, any basic lack of certainty over the concept of an Information Society or the reality of the Information Revolution should by no means prevent us from considering the possibilities of social change resulting from these trends. For one cannot rule out the possibility that the basic driving forces of the Information Revolution might yet trigger significant structural changes in the United States or other societies. And whether the portended transformations are truly revolutionary or simply part of the normal social evolutionary process, they are impacts nonetheless.

The primary focus of the widespread concern over the possibility of a revolutionary social transformation tended to be with such potential impacts, with what will be the end result of the transformation, whether it be revolutionary or evolutionary, into an information society. In other words, the fundamental issue has been the question of what will the Information Society look like. The future being notoriously difficult to research scientifically, most treatises have been based on the consideration of scenarios, or hypothetical considerations of what might be the final and end-state of the Information Revolution, given the continuation of current perceived trends and tendencies. The convoluted history of such concerns with the Information and related social revolutions have yielded a great number of such visions, ranging from the utopian to the dystopian. Still, there seem to be certain common threads identified within these disparate visions: massive shifts in employment patterns; development of large, integrated, information networks (or "information utilities"); and an increase in the scope of most organizations.

Most utopian visions foresee a future of great wealth, measured in terms of both material goods and quality of life, a wealth that is widely distributed in a society that has embodied the values of individualism, democracy, and equity. Such visions portray a world with open and equitable access to information of all kinds, a society whose focus has turned from material acquisition to the search for self-actualization. It is perceived as a truly international society that is synergistic, cooperative, democratic, and fully integrated. On the other hand, the dystopian visions have focused on images of massive structural unemployment and the development of a rigid class system based on the acquisition of certain (information-related) skills. The convergence of information technologies in such future worlds will have led to their use by authoritarian regimes to monitor and control captive populations. In such visions, information and access to it are tightly controlled and restricted, creating a new class division between the "haves" and the "have nots" in society. Such images have been provided most graphically by such writers as George Orwell in *1984* and Aldous Huxley in *Brave New World,* where a heavily centralized authoritarian regime monitors and controls almost every aspect of human life.

Although the promise of the "Information Society" may well be golden, reality rarely lives up to its potential for either positive or negative consequences. Anything that falls short of perfection, or its full positive potential, can be said to face problems of one sort or another. To the extent that potential problems may be discovered and addressed before they become ingrained in the developing social structure, they might be reduced or resolved by the implementation of directed policies. Any problematic aspects of social systems and structures are easier to correct before they, or their root causes, become a fundamental part of the basic structure of the new society and its organizational, political, and/or cultural systems; that is, before they become part of the genetic code of the Information Society. Thus, if the potential problem areas can be identified, considered, and perhaps even resolved before the problematic aspects of the transformation become firmly established in the new social structure, their negative impact might well be lessened or even avoided.

With this hope of avoiding the potential negative impacts of any social transformation in mind, the goal of this chapter is to try to identify some of the potential problem areas, and to consider the research addressing those issues. The differentiation between basic utopian and dystopian visions, and the range of problems addressed in the literature, can be said to deal primarily with two fundamental issues regarding how social systems deal with evolutionary pressures: (a) the impact of the various trends toward informationalization on work (reflecting both cultural and economic concerns), and (b) the issue of access to information and information technologies (reflecting primarily political and social equity concerns). How these issues are resolved in the process of social transformation (evolutionary or revolutionary) will have a profound impact on the nature of the resultant society.

WORK

The concerns over the impact of an Information Revolution on work have had two basic focuses. There has been the initial question of the impact of information technology, particularly computers, on employment levels and patterns in a society. Utopians foresaw huge employment opportunities in information and service sectors and the freeing of mankind from the drudgery of more basic physical labor. The focus of work, they argued, would shift from the exercise of physical power to mental skills. More pessimistic writers saw massive reduction in employment opportunities for unskilled workers and decreasing levels of employment in all sectors as the information technologies spread their labor-saving "benefits" throughout the economy. Dystopians also foresaw a growing distinction between skilled and unskilled labor based on the ability to acquire the information skills required for employment in the Information Society, which inevitably led to predictions of a rise of an underclass within the society.

There has also been a series of issues raised as to the likely influence of this transformation on the nature of work. (Bannon, Barry & Holst, 1982). On one hand, many early scenarios forecast an age of the "electronic cottage" where all work could be done at home using various information links, where workers were freed from repetitive drudgery and where increased productivity reduced working hours. Such treatments harped on the benefits such changes would have on the quality of life for information workers. On the other hand, concerns have been expressed about other, more negative, potential impacts of the Information Revolution. Concerns have been raised as to the effect of information technology (particularly VDTs) on health, the increased capacity for computer supervision and control of workers, and other "quality of life" issues such as the impact of the isolation of workers from both the product and each other.

Employment

Many scholars have expressed concern about the impact of the growth of computerization and information technologies on the level of employment in societies. Some (Theobald, 1981) have gone so far as to argue that unemployment would become so pervasive in the Information Age that alternatives must be found to satisfy the individual's perceived need to work and right to an income. The impact of automation, computer-aided manufacturing systems, and robotics has been widely predicted to lead to an elimination of unskilled jobs and the "deskilling" of many other jobs (Rada, 1980; Evans, 1983). The first of these two potential impacts is particularly problematic for many Third World societies, where most workers are unskilled, and there is generally a great need for increasing employment opportunities for the relatively unskilled. The "deskilling" of other kinds of jobs, however, may provide temporary alternatives for employment for those with little or no skills immediately appropriate to the new technologies.

It is usually agreed that the sector where employment opportunities are likely to actually grow is for those who are highly skilled, particularly in the tools of the Information Age. This immediately raises the question of the accessibility of training in such areas and skills, and the question of who should bear the social costs of retraining due to the obsolescence of industrial skills (Sieghart, 1981, Tonn, 1985). Studies of employment impacts in two U.S. states (Hudson & York, 1984; Schement, Lievrouw, & Dordick, 1983) have concluded that patterns in employment opportunities are changing, but educational systems do not seem to be prepared to turn out skilled information workers. Following the scenario predicted by many critics—an era of increasing specialization and the rise of a class-based social system based on such skills, which Galbraith (1971) termed the "technocracy"—these two studies predicted the rise of a large, undereducated minority, which could lead to the rise of a functional underclass in such social systems.

There are serious issues related to the employment impacts of any transition to an Information Society. Experience with past social transformations leads one to expect massive displacements in labor and radical shifts in employment patterns. To date, such displacements have followed the patterns of earlier Revolutions, with employment declines in one sector being more or less offset by increases in employment levels in alternative (service and information) sectors, where the impact of information technologies have yet to be fully felt. Whether such sectors will continue to be able to absorb displaced workers as the information technologies are more fully adopted in those sectors, or, as in the Industrial Revolution, a new economic sector will emerge to absorb displaced workers is still unknown. There is a strong fear among many scholars that problems related to employment effects have barely begun, and, unless addressed, these problems may result in the dystopian vision of a large degree of functional unemployment and the resulting creation of a new "underclass" with little or no opportunity for self-improvement.

Quality of Life

One of the basic potential negative impacts of the Information Revolution, which has been widely studied, is the impact of the diffusion and adoption of VDTs on the health of workers who use them. There have been general indications of various psycho-biological impacts of prolonged exposure to/use of computer terminals or VDTs (Cullen, 1982), although others have argued that any evidence of health hazard is not conclusive. Research is under way in many locations on the nature, severity, and cause of such adverse impacts on workers' health, and the results of such work may prove helpful to resolving any problems in this area.

A second issue, one which has been thought of variously as a positive and a negative impact, concerns the ability to work away from a centralized office or factory. Proponents (Espejo & Ziv, 1982; Inose, 1984) speak of the facilitation and strengthening of communities of interest, those that are not determined by their employment-imposed geographical limitations and the employment opportunities created by information technologies for those whose mobility is restricted. These advantages are often linked to a movement in employment away from urban centers and a greater opportunity to engage in desired non-work activities. On the other hand, there is increasing concern about the effect of the isolation of workers from their colleagues, as well as the process of creating a discernable product. A second concern has been with the increased capacity for control and supervision of employees and workloads afforded by diffusion of computerized information systems in the workplace (Evans, 1983).

One of the most widely held positive impacts of the social transformation to an Information Society is the development of a new set of "post-materialistic" basic social values (Cherns, 1980; Masuda, 1980, 1982). Scholars have foreseen increases in individualization (Ploman, 1975), egalitarianism (Nora & Minc, 1981), time-value (Masuda, 1981), and social solidarity (Becker, 1983; Takasaki, 1978), all leading to a new conceptualization of value and worth, removed from the acquisition of material goods and based on more synergistic or cooperative efforts rather than a sense of competition. Many of the policies undertaken to promote the rise of Information Societies in France and Japan were found to promote or mirror such value shifts (Bates, 1988). The issue facing scholars, however, is not only what new values, attitudes, and behaviours (Williams, Rice, & Dordick, 1985) might emerge, but what should be done in the period of transformation to identify and preserve desirable values and the social structures embodying those values (Cater, 1981).

ACCESS

Three basic issues have been raised with regard to the question of access to information and information technologies. One potential impact of the Information Revolution foreseen in most treatments is the formation of what has been called information utilities: massive information storage, retrieval, and transmission systems based on integration of computer and telecommunication networks. The issues that have risen with regard to information utilities deal with the question of what information is placed in the net and who controls access to either the system as a whole, or subsets of it and the information contained within. In plainer terms, the issues raised are those of privacy, equity, and censorship.

Censorship

Censorship in this context refers to the potential to restrict or deny access to information, to interfere with what many would call the right to information and to be informed. Many considerations of the potential for development of an Information Society within the Soviet block (Stonier, 1983) have focused on that society's need to maintain censorship, that is, strict controls over access to information of certain types, contrasted with the gains in knowledge and science promoted through a free exchange of ideas and information. They have noted the discrepancy between the ideals of information access and the reality of authoritarian politics with its inherent need to control information and its conduits.

Generally, scholars have been concerned not only with the economic nonoptimality of restrictions on the accessibility of information (i.e. censorship) but with the question of the power which is inherently conferred with the capacity to deny access to information to others (Craig, 1979). Information and access to information are becoming increasingly necessary to cope with modern life and to be able to be effective not only politically (Nimmo, 1985) but economically and socially. Being able to control access to information, to limit the options of the user either economically or politically, grants to those who control access a degree of control or power over that user. To the degree that such potential power is exercised by one group over another creates questions of equity.

Equity

One of the fundamental issues facing scholars examining the Information Society, one likely to have major impacts on both economic and political systems, is the problem of the degree of differential access to information and information systems imposed by either monetary or nonmonetary costs facing potential users (MacRae, 1970). That is, there has been considerable concern about the transition to an information society influencing the distribution of power both within and between societies, based in part on differential access to information. Utopian visions are generally based on the assumption that there would be few, if any, restrictions or limits placed on the access by individuals to the full stock of information and knowledge in the society.

On the other hand, it has been argued (Blake, 1978; Garnham, 1982; Mosco, 1982) that the current class-based social system is likely to replicate itself as information and information technologies are industrialized and as access is controlled by the ability to pay. This problematic aspect of the Information Society, the potential for the co-option of information technology by commercial interests, has been regularly addressed in recent years by Schiller (1981, 1983, 1984, 1985) in his concern over the "privatization" of information. Similarly, other scholars, building on a tradition of research of Information Gaps (Tichenor, Olien, & Donohue, 1970), have been concerned with the possibility that the gaps between the information rich and the information poor is apt to increase in the Information Society, and thus the result will not be a radical social transformation, but a continuation of a class-based capitalistic, economics-focused system.

Not all concerns, however, are with the impact of differentiation based only on economic costs. Brzezinski (1971, p. 164) noted that "power will gravitate into the hands of those who control the information and correlate it most rapidly;" those who have access to the developing information networks and can make most efficient use of the data that such networks can provide. There is the potential problem that those who control information systems may control access to them, an issue that has already been raised with respect to current media (Haight, 1979) as well as the developing technologies (O'Brien & Helleiner, 1980; Dervin, 1982).

Privacy

The issue of privacy has arisen in recent years with the increase in the number and scope of various administrative systems that have been facilitated by advances in information technologies. There is, today, an enormous capacity to collect and store information on individuals. Several scholars have noted the capacity of some of the two-way cable systems to collect information not only on viewing patterns, but on other uses (Wicklein, 1981). But the capacity for intrusion is not limited to such esoteric information systems: Modern telephone exchanges are capable of tracking and noting every call made, and electronic banking systems (including the ubiquitous credit card) are capable of tracking most expenditures. Insurance, credit, and government agencies have routinely collected immense amounts of what is usually considered to be personal information. The growing linkage of these systems has not only increased the capacity to gather, correlate, and analyze information of a personal nature, but to make the purposive use of that information in a negative manner increasingly possible.

The inherent capacity for the invasion of privacy posed by such systems has led to the adoption of privacy legislation in several countries. The Organization for Economic Cooperation and Development (OECD) has proposed guidelines in an attempt to balance the need to protect the privacy of individuals and the need to promote a free flow of information (Martin-Lof, 1982), although concern has been expressed over the effectiveness of such efforts in forestalling the perceived trend to mass surveillance (Lenk, 1983). Restricting the collection or dissemination of such information, however, can also have a negative impact, providing a basis for limiting access to other types of information. There is a fine line between privacy and censorship to be trod in the formation of the Information Society.

POLITICAL IMPLICATIONS

The utopian view of the information society is one of increasing democratization and a reduction in authoritarianism, both socially and politically. Masuda (1981, 1982) foresaw the rise of a participatory democracy, based on agreement, self-restraint, and synergy. Others, as discussed before, have noted the great potential in the rise of information systems for surveillance, control through censorship, and the possibility of a social transformation resulting in an authoritarian regime rather than a participatory democracy. Where a society will fall in this continuum would seem to be based on the level of participation allowed or encouraged in the system and the degree of centralized control permitted any individual or group.

With respect to the issue of the level of basic participation in the system, Michael (1971) noted that even if developing information systems are used to enhance participation in democratic decision making, the use of such systems may well require skills or impose costs that which effectively prohibit participation by all members of the society. The issue of equity and level of participation within the system are probably linked to the likelihood that the information society realized within a culture is apt to reflect more closely utopian or dystopian visions.

A number of other issues of a somewhat political nature have been raised by some scholars. Some writers (Martin-Lof, 1982; Valaskakis, 1982) have raised the issue of the vulnerability of a sophisticated, highly integrated and interdependent technological system dependent on the ready and constant supply of electricity to either accident or sabotage. A second potential problem of vulnerability is the prospect of information systems and data banks resident outside the boundaries of one society being held hostage by the host society. A further issue raised is the specter of cultural pollution and the related problems of maintaining cultural identities in a rapidly integrating and internationaliz-ing society (Ganley, 1981; Sieghart, 1981). A few scholars (Inose, 1984), on the other hand, have noted the capacity of information technology to preserve and protect indigenous culture, at least in a recorded form.

CONCLUSION

As demonstrated only briefly in this review, there are a considerable number of issues facing those who think about, or seek to influence, the development of an Information Society. Current trends in the development, diffusion, and adoption of information technologies and systems said to form the foundation for such a society, present myriad opportunities for the development of a particular kind of society or culture. What kind of society that will evolve depends on the choices made today and tomorrow—on how the issues discussed in this paper are coped with.

One could, of course, simply sit back and watch the various forces work themselves out and hope that they manage to deal satisfactorily with the potential for both good and evil presented by the concept In-formation Society. Or, we can attempt to address the issues firmly, and take steps to enhance the likelihood that the more utopian views of an information age will come to pass. Although the transformation to an Information Society is yet incomplete, the opportunity to try to guide that transition and development still exists; but once the time for choices is past, and the resulting fundamental patterns for social structures becomes ingrained and self-regenerative, they become resistant to change, for better or worse. Then we are more or less stuck with whatever social system emerges.

REFERENCES

Bannon, L., Barry, U., & Holst, O. (1982). Information Technology: *Impact on the way of life.* Dublin: Tycooly International.

Bates, B. J. (1984, May). *Conceptualizing the information society: The search for a definition of social attributes.* Paper presented at the International Communication Association Conference, San Francisco, CA.

Bates, B. J. (1988). The role of social values in information policy: The case of France and Japan. In B. D. Ruben (Ed.), *Information and behavior.* Volume 2. New Brunswick, NJ: Transaction.

Becker, J. (1983). Contradictions in the informationalization of politics and society. *Gazette,* 32(2), 103–118.

Bell, D. (1973). *The coming of the post-industrial society.* New York: Basic Books.

Benedetti, M. (1980). European telecommunications-plan for the future. *Telecommunications Policy,* 4(2), 150–152.

Beniger, J. (1986). *The control revolution: Technological and economic origins of the information society.* Cambridge, MA: Harvard University Press.

Blake, F. M. (1978). Public access to information in the post-industrial society. In E. J. Josey (Ed.), *The Information Society: Issues and Answers.* Phoenix, AZ: Oryx Press.

Boorstein, D. (1978). *The republic of technology.* New York: Harper and Row.

Bowes, J. E. (1981). Japan's approach to an information society: A critical perspective. In G. C. Wilhoit & H. DeBuck (Eds.), *Mass communication review yearbook, Volume 2.* Beverly Hills, CA: Sage.

Bowes, J. E., Sullivan, C. B., & Wheeler, T. J. (1985, May). *From agricultural to information: Bypassing the industrial revolution in Ireland.* Paper presented at the International Communication Association Conference, Honolulu, HI.

Branco, P. J. C. (1982). *Brazil and the information society of the twenty-first century.* In H. F. Didsbury, Jr. (Ed.), *Communications and the future.* Bethesda, MD: World Future Society.

Brzezinski, Z. (1970). Between two ages: America's role in the technetronic age. New York: Viking Press.

Brzezinski, Z. (1971). Moving into a Technetronic Society. In A. F. Westin (Ed.), *Information technology in a democracy.* Cambridge, MA: Harvard University Press.

Cater, D. (1981). Human values in the information society. In C. C. Rochell (Ed.), *An information agenda for the 1980s.* Chicago: American Library Association.

Cherns, A. (1980). Work and values: Shifting patterns in industrial society. *International Social Science Journal, 32*(3), 427–441.

Craig, A. (1979). Information and politics: Towards greater government intervention? *International Journal, 34*(2), 209–226.

Cullen, J. (1982). Impact of Information technology on Human Well-being. In L. Bannon, U. Barry, & O. Holst (Eds.), *Information technology: Impact on the way of life.* Dublin: Tycooly International Publishing.

Cullen, R. B. (1985, May). *Telecom 2010: A comment on the development of telecommunications in Australia.* Paper presented at the International Communication Association Conference, Honolulu, HI.

Dervin, B. (1982). Citizen access as an information equity issue. In J. R. Schement, F. Gutierrez, & M. A. Sirbu, *Telecommunication policy handbook.* New York: Praeger.

Dizard, W. P., Jr. (1982). *The coming information age.* New York: Longman.

Ellul, J. (1964). *The technological society,* transl. John Wilkinson. New York: Alfred A. Knopf.

Espejo, M. R., & Ziv, J. (1982). Communication, delocalization of work and everyday life. In L. Bannon, U. Barry, & O. Holst (Eds.), *Information technology: Impact on the way of life.* Dublin: Tycooly International Publishing.

Evans, J. (1983). The worker and the workplace. In G. Friedrichs & A. Schaff (Eds.), *Microelectronics and society: A report to the club of Rome.* New York: Mentor.

Galbraith, J. K. (1971). *The new industrial state,* 2nd rev. ed. Boston: Houghton-Mifflin.

Ganley, O. H. (1981). Political aspects of communications and information resources in Canada. *The Information Society, 1*(1), 79–89.

Garnham, N. (1982). The information society is also a class society. In L. Bannon, U. Barry, & O. Holst (Eds.), *Information technology: Impact on the way of life.* Dublin: Tycooly International Publishing.

Haight, T. R., Ed. (1979). *Telecommunications policy and the citizen.* New York: Praeger.

Hudson, H. E., & York, L. (1984, May). *The growth of the information sector in Texas.* Paper presented to the International Communication Association Conference, San Francisco, CA.

Inose, H. (1984). Challenges for policy of network oriented society: A Japanese view. *Information Economics and Policy, 1*(4), 369–379.

Jussawalla, M., & Cheah, C. (1983). Toward an information economy: The case of Singapore. *Information Economics and Policy, 1*(2), 161–176.

Karunaratne, N. D. (1984). Planning for the Australian information economy. *Information Economics and Policy*, 1(4), 345–367.

Lamberton, D. M., Ed. (1974). The information revolution. *Annals of the American Academy of Political and Social Science*, Vol. 412. Philadelphia: American Academy of Political and Social Science.

Langdale, J. (1984). Computerization in Singapore and Australia. *The Information Society*, 3(2), 131–153.

Lenk, K. (1983). Information technology and society. In G. Friedrichs & A. Schaff (Eds.), *Micro-electronics and society: A report to the club of Rome*. New York: Mentor.

Machlup, F. (1962). *The production and distribution of knowledge in the United States*. Princeton, NJ: Princeton University Press.

MacRae, Duncan, Jr. (1970). Some political choices in the development of communications technology. In H. Sackman & N. Nie (Eds.), *The information utility and social choice*. Montvale, NJ: AFIPS Press.

Martin-Lof, J. (1982). Some policy issues in the international debate. In L. Bannon, U. Barry, & O. Holst (Eds.), *Information technology: Impact on the way of life*. Dublin: Tycooly International Publishing.

Masuda, Y. (1981). *The information society as post-industrial society*. Bethesda, MD: World Future Society.

Masuda, Y. (1982). Vision of the Global Information Society. In L. Bannon, U. Barry, & O. Holst (Eds.), *Information technology: Impact on the way of life*. Dublin: Tycooly International Publishing.

McLuhan, M. (1964). *Understanding Media: The extensions of man*. New York: McGraw-Hill.

Michael, D. N. (1971). Democratic participation and technological planning. In A. F. Westin (Ed.), *Information technology in a democracy*. Cambridge, MA: Harvard University Press.

Mosco, V. (1982). *Pushbutton fantasies: Critical perspectives on videotex and information technology*. Norwood, NJ: Ablex.

Nimmo, D. (1985). Information and political behavior. In B. D. Ruben (Ed.), *Information and behavior. Volume 1*. New Brunswick, NJ: Transaction.

Nora, S., & Minc, A. (1980). *Computerization and society*. Boston: MIT Press.

O'Brien, R. C., & Helleiner, G. K. (1980). The political economy of information in a changing international economic order. *International Organization*, 34(4), 445–470.

Parker, E. B. (1981). Information services and economic growth. *The Information Society*, 1(1), 71–78.

Ploman, E. W. (1975). Information as environment. *Journal of Communication*, 25(2), 93–97.

Porat, M. U. (1977). *The information economy*. Washington, DC: U.S. Department of Commerce.

Porat, M. U. (1978). Global implications of an information society. *Journal of Communication*, 28(1), 70–80.

Rada, J. F. (1980). Microelectronics and information technology: A challenge for research in the social sciences. *Social Science Information*, 19(2), 435–465.

Salvaggio, J. L. (1983). Social problems of information societies: The U.S. and Japanese experiences. *Telecommunications Policy*, 7(3), 228–242.

Schement, J. R., Lievrouw, L. A., & Dordick, H. S. (1983). The information society in California: Social factors influencing its emergence. *Telecommunications Policy*, 7(1), 64–72.

Schiller, H. I. (1981). *Who knows: Information in the age of the fortune 500*. Norwood, NJ: Ablex.

Schiller, H. I. (1983). The privatization of information. In E. Wartella & D. C. Whitney, (Eds.), *Mass communication review yearbook, volume 4*. Beverly Hills, CA: Sage.

Schiller, H. I. (1984). *Information and the crises economy*. Norwood, NJ: Ablex.

Schiller, H. I. (1985). Privatizing the public sector: The information connection. In B. D. Ruben, (Ed.), *Information and behavior, Volume 1*. New Brunswick, NJ: Transaction.

Sieghart, P. (1981). The international implications of the development of microelectronics. *The Information Society, 1*(1), 1–15.

Snow, M. (1985). Policy questions in economic regulation of information societies: Evidence from Japan, the U.S., and other industrialized nations. *KEIO Communication Review, 6.*

Stonier, T. (1983). The microelectronic revolution, Soviet political structure, and the future of East/West relations. *Political Quarterly, 54*(2), 137–151.

Takasaki, N. (1978). The quest for 'quality of life' for an information society. In A. S. Edelstein, J. E. Bowes, & S. M. Harsel (Eds.), *Information societies: Comparing the Japanese and American experiences.* Seattle: International Communication Center.

Theobald, R. (1981). *Beyond despair: A policy guide to the communications era.* Revised Ed. Cabin John, MD: Seven Locks Press.

Tichenor, P. J., Olien, C. N., & Donohue, G. A. (1970). Mass media flow and differential growth in knowledge. *Public Opinion Quarterly, 34,* 159–179.

Tonn, B. E. (1985). Information technology and society: Prospects and problems. *The Information Society, 3*(3), 241–260.

Valaskakis, K. (1982). The concept of infomediation: A framework for a structural interpretation of the information revolution. In L. Bannon, U. Barry, & O. Holst (Eds.), *Information technology: Impact on the way of life.* Dublin: Tycooly International Publishing.

Wicklein, J. (1981). *The electronic nightmare: The home communications set and your freedom.* Boston: Beacon Press.

Williams, F., Rice, R. E., & Dordick, H. S. (1985). Behavioral impacts in the information age. In B. D. Ruben (Ed.), *Information and behavior. Volume 1.* New Brunswick, NJ: Transaction.

3 The Origins of the Information Society in the United States: Competing Visions

JORGE REINA SCHEMENT
Rutgers University

Behind the Thomson and Homestead and Keystone plants were the famous Lucy and Carrie furnaces for making pig iron; and behind them was the enormous Henry Clay Frick Coke Company with its 40,000 acres of coal land, its 2,688 railway cars, and its 13,252 coking ovens; and behind this in turn were 244 miles of railways (organized into three main companies) to ship materials to and from the coking ovens; and then at a still more distant remove were a shipping company and a dock company with a fleet of Great Lakes ore-carrying steamers; and then at the very point of origin of the steel-making process, was the Oliver Mining Company with its great mines in Michigan and Wisconsin. (Heilbroner, 1977, p. 95)

World satellite systems now make distance and time irrelevant. We witness and react to crises simultaneously with their happening. Networks of telephones, telex, radio, and television have exponentially increased the *density* of human contact. More people can be in touch with one another during any single day in the new communications environment than many did in a lifetime in the fourteenth century. The convergence of telecommunications and computing technologies distribute information automation to the limits of the world's communication networks. We are well past the point of having the capability to transform most of human knowledge into electronic form for access at any point on the earth's surface. (Williams, 1982, p. 230)

Heilbroner's panorama evokes an image of industrial America that is still familiar because it links America's present to its past. The sec

29

ond image from Williams has gained familiarity more recently; it associates the present with the future. It portrays America as an information society.

The idea of a modern information society is rooted in two concepts. Fritz Machlup first introduced the notion of a knowledge economy as a result of his analysis of the contribution of information activities to the 1958 U.S. Gross National Product (Machlup, 1962). The second concept stems from Daniel Bell's interpretation of a large service sector as the hallmark of "post-industrial society" (Bell, 1973).

Information society is a powerful idea precisely because it provokes the imagination. To Americans concerned about the direction of their society, it proposes a future that is exotic, but increasingly familiar; the mystery of computers is giving way to the presence of PCs in the family study. To economists, communications researchers, and information scientists, it provides a framework for interpreting patterns of culture and behavior. The notion of the "information economy," for example, encouraged economists to consider information as a good exchanged in the marketplace, and to ponder its contribution to the GNP. Likewise, the idea of information work has led sociologists and communications researchers to reconsider the roles of information technologies in everyday life. The opening of conceptual territory has led to a great deal of speculation and theorizing.

Social scientists have identified an enormous range of phenomena related to the uses of information. Understandably, they disagree over the interpretation of certain statistics. Consequently, the literature documenting these patterns is growing rapidly (a recent bibliography includes 479 entries [Schement, Parker, & Shelton, 1985]). Despite the diversity of findings, the literature reflects six recurring themes:

1. **Informational materialism, or information exchanged as an economic commodity.** Information has been exchanged in the marketplace since ancient times, but it has played a secondary role to the traffic in "real" physical commodities (Braudel, 1979). Now it is a primary commodity itself, bought and sold in volumes that rival manufactured goods and agricultural commodities.

2. **A large information workforce.** Information manipulation predominates the productive time of a significant proportion of the workforce. Individuals perform information work in a wide variety of occupations where the main tasks are the production, recycling, or maintenance of information and/or information technology (Schement & Lievrouw, 1984).

3. **Interconnectedness among individuals and institutions.** Traditional distinctions between information technologies and their related institu-

tional functions have faded. The increased interconnection of technologies has greatly enhanced the movement of information among institutions (eg. banks, credit card companies, stock brokerage houses), and indeed, there are fewer differences today in what these institutions do. But more importantly, the interconnection of technologies and institutional roles has allowed some industrial era institutions to transform themselves into new configurations that facilitate information movement and manipulation in order to maximize their profits.

4. The special status of scientific knowledge. Scientists still pursue knowledge for its own sake. But they also pursue knowledge in a context that values science as a commercial resource, which enhances the advantage of corporations and government. In this setting, the stakes are too high to be left entirely to instinct, and science is increasingly directed by private sector institutions and values.

5. A social environment with many messages and channels. The media constitute a pervasive presence in the modern social environment. The superabundance of messages and channels in American life, bring with them a daunting array of content and advertising and have become an important basis for interpreting reality (Schudson, 1984).

6. Widely diffused information technology. Technologies that enable individuals to manipulate, more, or store information have been incorporated as a compelling theme across all descriptions of the information society. The machines that embody that technology, are the visible icons of social change (Ellul, 1964).

FROM PATTERNS TO EXPLANATIONS

Since the end of World War II, social observers have noted the importance of various informational activities. Derek J. de Solla Price surveyed the growth of "big science" in the 1950s. At the end of his administration, Dwight Eisenhower warned the nation against the alliance of science with industry and the military (Price, 1963; Eisenhower, 1971). Even then, there was evidence of the commercial exchange of information and of the presence of information work, suggesting the importance of such activities. Machlup thought so in 1962, when he noted

> As an economy develops and as a society becomes more complex, efficient organization of production, trade, and government seems to require an increasing degree of division of labor between knowledge production and physical production. A quite remarkable increase in the division of

labor between 'brain work' and largely physical performance has occurred in all sectors of our economic and social organization. (p. 6)

The significance of these patterns stems from the social relations they imply. To Bell, the patterns suggested that the characteristics and driving forces he observed comprised a new society that must be fundamentally different from the industrial era. He argued that the postwar growth of informational activities was conclusive evidence that industrial society was giving way to a "post-industrial" society. Indeed, many information scientists describe the information society as post-industrial, believing that revolutionary social changes are in progress.

Scholars who support a post-industrial interpretation have at times seemed ready to close the book on industrial society (Crawford, 1983; Dizard, 1982; Ochai, 1984; Williams, 1982). But they would be hasty.

Compelling though the contemporary evidence might be, it leaves important questions unanswered: What gives rise to an information society? Has the industrial framework of society given way to some other, newer form of social organization? If so, what are its characteristics? Can an information society also be industrial? Does capitalism continue to play a role in the growth of informational activities? We must pursue the answers to each of these questions, in order to determine whether we have evidence of: (a) a post-industrial society that has truly broken with the structures and social relations of the industrial age, or (b) a new era of industrial society that is oriented to information (Dizard, 1982; Douglas & Guback, 1984; Hammer, 1976; Malik, 1981; Meehan, 1984; Schiller, 1981; Slack, 1984; Williams, 1982).

These two interpretations imply that there are at least two different frameworks for evaluating the same patterns of informational activities. Similarly, they imply different sets of hypotheses. Ultimately, each creates the basis for a different paradigm to set the conceptual foundation for thinking about the information society. Without resolving the question of origin, scholars lack the long-term perspective necessary to build a theory that accounts for the pervasiveness and diversity of information activities in modern society.

In this article, I propose that the information society is rooted in the growth of capitalism and in the expansion of industrialism in the United States. Furthermore, these roots are evidence of continuity with industrial society, rather than discontinuity. Therefore, I reject the characterization of information society as post-industrial and contend that it is more accurately a society oriented to the industrial production and distribution of information.

THE LOGIC OF THE DEBATE

A logical resolution of the question of origins depends on the following premises:

1. The influence of capitalism, which played an indispensible role in the rise of industrialism, must first be determined in order to resolve any question of industrialism versus post-industrialism.
2. If post-industrial society is to be considered the successor to industrial society, then it must be shown that the framework within which change occurs (that is, the primary social forces driving industrial society) has given way to a different framework which shapes post-industrial society.

The key to understanding any social change, information society included, is in determining its major influences or causes. For example, to argue that the ascendance of informational activities constitutes sufficient evidence for the passing of industrial society is to assume that such activities result from a different set of social forces than those which formed industrial society. But the same set of social forces can result in varied outcomes, especially over a long period of time. Because industrial society spans 200 years, it is important to recognize the possibility that the industrial revolution might have led to the present emphasis on information.

If there are new social forces whose existence has prompted the growth of informational activities, then there is indeed a basis for proposing that information society is post-industrial. On the other hand, the continuing influence of the determinants of industrial society on the pattern of information uses would indicate a strong connection between industrial and the informational society.

TWO CONFLICTING VIEWS OF THE INFORMATION SOCIETY

Information Society as Post-Industrial

Breaking with the past is a popular image in the literature that explores changes in the 20th century. By choosing *The Age of Discontinuity* as his title, Drucker (1969) took change as his basic premise. Bell (1973) resolved the question of continuity by forecasting *The Coming of Post-Industrial Society.* Williams (1982) chose the disjunctive phrase communications revolution, and others have similarly described recent changes in society (Forestor, 1981; Nora & Minc, 1980; Toffler, 1980). Dizard (1982) justified his title, *The Coming Information Age*, by identifying a new stage of socio-economic development.

> The resources are so pervasive and influential that it is now becoming clear the United States is moving into a new era—the information age. Ours is the first nation to complete the three-stage shift from an agricultural society to an industrial one and to a society whose new patterns are only now emerging. (p. 2).

As articulated by Dizard, this is the gist of the post-industrial position. The prevalence of informational activities seems to prove that a revolutionary social change has taken place.

Bell's conception of a post-industrial society forms the foundation for the idea that a new "information society" has replaced industrial society. According to this view, the rate of technological and social change has increased to the point where a genuine discontinuity has occurred. Consequently, the United States, as the second industrial nation, becomes the first information society.

Five basic assumptions are implied in this interpretation:

1. Industrial society, and its forms of social organization are believed to have largely passed. Proponents describe new products, industries, classes, and social relations.

2. The sheer volume of informational activities validates the idea of a post-industrial society. Not all scholars pay equal attention to all kinds of activities. However, they have amassed much empirical evidence to document the existence of these kinds of activities.

3. A post-industrial interpretation assumes sequential societal development. All the world's nations presumably travel a single evolutionary path, from hunting and gathering to informational. By proclaiming the dawn of a new era, the post-industrial view draws a parallel with evolutionary social theories, such as Walt Rostow's stages of economic growth (Rostow, 1963, 1971).[1] Broadly speaking, we may imagine post-industrial society as the culmination of human cultural maturity, the sixth stage of economic growth, or as Nora and Minc (1981) exult, the ultimate civilization.

4. Most of the literature explains the growth of informational activities outside of a historical framework. Only Bell reviews the period of industrialization, though his critics have accused him of being a selective historian (Harrington, 1977; Stearns, 1977). The rest of the literature accepts Bell's proposition that great discontinuities occur during periods

[1]In *The World Economy,* Rostow rejects the idea of a post-industrial society and holds to his original theory of five stages.

of high rates of change, concluding, like Dizard, that changes in information retrieval and distribution must be fundamental. As a result of this historical perspective, the literature focuses on the future (Bell's book is subtitled, *A Venture in Social Forecasting*) rather than on the relationship of the present to the past.

5. None of these writers predict the withering away of capitalism. They assume that post-industrial society replaces the industrial era while capitalism remains undisturbed. Bell foresaw a new capitalist society where technocratic efficiency would dominate policy (though Harrington (1977) has pointed out that any society where social goals supercede the economic function is also post-capitalist). Bell himself (1973) is unclear on this point, and other authors seem to treat capitalism as mere background noise for the information revolution.

Considerable research has followed Bell's initial premise. What we know of the patterns of informational activities has grown from researchers who built on the post-industrial theme. But they have not substantially added to Bell's theory, so that his original interpretation remains the dominant context for thinking about information and society.

Information Society as Unmodified Capitalism

Schiller first criticized the post-industrial view in *Who Knows* (1981). He rejected any attribution of uniqueness to the pattern of informational activities and charged that the entire information society idea could be understood within the framework of the processes that have characterized American capitalism. He documented the transfer of information from the public sector to the private sector and showed that the transfer has been motivated by capitalist values. This "privatization of information" leading to a greater concentration of ownership among large American corporations, has developed along the same lines experienced in other noninformational industries. Moreover, he maintained that this trend could not be the result of the computer revolution, or any other recent technological development.[2]

In his analysis of teletext, Mosco (1982) continued Schiller's argument and pointed out that the characteristics of post-industrial/information society permit increased control of the labor process, a relationship closely associated with the evolution of capitalism. He criticized enthusiasts for selling "tinny visions of utopia" and for ignoring the negative consequences of capitalist development. Like Schiller, he con-

---

[2]Criticisms of post-industrialism surfaced even before Bell published his book and have persisted. See Ssewczyk (1970), Heilbroner (1973), Stearns (1974), and Lisy (1984).

cluded that much of what goes under the rubric of the information society can be explained as part of the progress of capitalism.

Douglas and Guback (1984) reviewed the same literature and questioned one of its basic assumptions, the idea that information society is revolutionary. They argued that the term "revolution" is poorly understood in the literature where it is often used as a buzz word. They rejected the claim that information may replace capital as a primary resource. Indeed, they found no evidence that historically significant social relationships, such as the class struggle, have disappeared. Douglas and Guback criticized information economists for focusing on information as output, rather than as part of the social process, thereby confusing imaginary revolutionary change with the effects of capitalism. Like Schiller and Mosco, they explained all information activities as resulting from the forces of capitalism, implying that there is no such thing as an informationally oriented society.

Meehan's "third vision" (1984) is less extreme, criticizing both optimistic and pessimistic visions of the information society. She is as uneasy with those who predict a computerized utopia of electronic cottages as she is with those who envision and Orwellian dystopia of masses of information poor watched over by Big Brother. She disagrees with the excessive negativism of Schiller and Mosco, but does not reject their view of unmodified capitalism. Meehan maintains that analysts like Schiller and Mosco have improperly interpreted the dynamics of capitalist forces and the social conditions they create. She therefore predicts that life in a future information society will be just as boring and tedious as it is now, "an ordinary dystopia of material relationships driven by the momentum of traditional capitalist values" (p. 257–271).

THE NEED FOR A THIRD INTERPRETATION

Bell's post-industrial society (and his implicit assumptions) constitute the foundation of most studies that focus on informational activities in society. But as a theory of the information society, it contains several weaknesses.

In the first place, writers adopting Bell's point of view have shown little concern over proposing a fundamental shift so soon after the previous one. The industrial revolution was in full swing into the last decades of the nineteenth century; only a century later, another equally momentous revolution is already being hypothesized. Aside from the logical problems created by positing a social model based on ever increasing rates of change, taking this position also requires an overly narrow view of industrial society. In the literature, it is usually defined by its earliest technology. By contrast, inventions of the 20th century (computers, satellites) seem "post-industrial."

By arguing that an increase in the *rate* of change constitutes a societal revolution, change is confounded with the context in which it occurs. For a revolution to actually occur, the basis for social organization—the very context of the change—must shift. What Bell and others overlook, is that capitalism was and is a context which encourages certain kinds of change. Thus, industrial entrepreneurs sought higher profits by concentrating on the process of industrialization, through the growth of firms, economies of scale in production, increased productivity, deskilled labor, and mechanization. They certainly sought profits by encouraging social change. These tendencies appear as surely today in the "new" computer industry, in virtually all of the same forms. But the post-industrial/information society literature has confused the products of change with the process and context of change.

If the logic of post-industrialism is weak, then why is its appeal so strong? It may be that post-industrialism reinforces the common cultural belief held by Americans that they are somehow exempt from the course of history, that they live in special times. Certainly, academics and professionals in fields such as information science, computer science, systems analysis, communications, engineering, and management, who have led the way in computer use, seem willing to assume that the technological transformation in information retrieval is also a fundamental revolution altering the social fabric.

The critiques led by Schiller have brought questions concerning the processes and effects of capitalism to a literature that has largely focused on building scenarios of the future. The value of this criticism lies in addressing a glaring omission. Thus, Schiller, Mosco, and others provide a basis for testing the assertions made by supporters of the post-industrial idea.

However, in focusing on the omissions of post-industrialism, the critics have overlooked its primary focus. They can explain the role played by capitalism in the formation of the pattern of informational activities, but they are unable to distinguish the relative influence of industrialization, apart from capitalism. By examining only the dynamics of capitalism, their critique remains incomplete.

The two arguments do not actually oppose each other; rather their directions are skewed. Each addresses what the other ignores. The advocates of post-industrialism hold that new social relations emerge as the old ones of the industrial era fade. The group of critics led by Schiller argue that social relations characteristic of capitalism continue to dominate society. To move the discussion beyond this bipolar debate, the interactions among industrialism, capitalism, and the pattern of informational activities must be resolved.[3]

Capitalism and the Sale of Information

The purchase and sale of information as a commodity is the most visible of the information activities. Proponents of the post-industrial view have pondered the peculiarities of information commodities as compared to material commodities, whereas critics have been alarmed at the ease with which information has been adapted to the requirements of advanced capitalism.

Simply put, capitalism is an economic order based on the profit motive and founded on the right of the individual to own private property. It is characterized by the continual accumulation of material wealth, in the pursuit of profit. In capitalist societies, individuals are likely to devote considerable energy to exploring ways to get rich. Moreover, they do not measure their wealth simply by the extent of their private property, but by the capital value or worth of that property (Baran & Sweezy, 1966; Hacker, 1940; Heilbroner & Singer, 1984; Katz, Doucet, & Stern, 1982).

These two characteristics, private property and the pursuit of profit, are clearly the driving forces behind the conversion of information into a commodity. Economically, the history of the United States is the story of individuals who sought to convert the nation's many resources into private property, in order to gain wealth from them. The widespread commoditization of information is the most recent part of this story, but the seeds of commoditization were sown early in the nation's history.

Members of the Constitutional Convention gave the U.S. Congress the power to promote science and the "useful arts"; therefore, they guaranteed inventors and authors exclusive rights to their discoveries and writings (Department of Commerce, 1981). Congress passed the first patent law in 1790. It expressed the legislators' beliefs that man has a natural property right to his ideas, that society should reward citizens for useful ideas, and that an inventor should only surrender his secret knowledge in return for society's protection (Machlup, 1958). The entire United States now conformed to a trend begun in 1641, when

---

[3]I am indebted to my fellow members of the informal seminar on the information society, at the Graduate School of Library and Information Science, UCLA, and especially to Hal Borko for helping me clarify the issues in this debate.

[4]*The Story of the United States Patent and Trademark Office,* p. v. He invented a new way of making salt.

General Court granted Samuel Winslow the first patent in North America.[4]

But even while they asserted their commitment to the supremacy of individual property, the founders recognized the contradictions. As followers of Adam Smith, they believed in the evil of monopolies. Yet they accepted "temporary monopolies" in order to reward inventors for their contributions and to compensate them for their risk and expense (Machlup, 1958; Smith, 1902). Furthermore, they understood the irony of complaints that something had been stolen which the inventor still possessed (Machlup, 1958).

When they considered the written word, the framers of the constitution went one step further and wrote the first copyright law with a commitment to both views. The copyright statute of 1790 attempted to reconcile two opposing principles: access, the freest possible dissemination of knowledge, versus economic costs, restrictions to protect intellectual property (Seltzer, 1978). It laid the basis for the growth of publishing.

Because the first amendment to the constitution guaranteed freedom of the press, 19th-century newspaper publishers wrote without fear of government censorship. Their views were varied and impassioned. But their principal interest lay in the sale of their newspapers. The *New York Sun*, whose masthead declared "It Shines for All," claimed a circulation of 50,000 by 1851. It shared New York (population 515,547[5]) with four other penny dailies and ten sixpenny papers (Schiller, 1981). Their success in the first half of the 19th-century established commercial foundations for the dissemination of information.

The profit motive encouraged further implementation of information technology, though disapproving voices were hardly silent. Samuel F. B. Morse, inventor of the telegraph, wished to avoid privatization, "For myself, I should prefer that the government should possess the invention, although pecuniary interests of the proprietors induce them to lean towards arrangements with private companies."[6] Accordingly, the government completed a line from Washington to Baltimore in 1844. The commercial potential was obvious and Congress soon leased the line to the Magnetic Telegraph Company (Thompson, 1947). The pattern was set.

Thirty years later, Alexander Graham Bell sought commercial exploitation from the moment of his earliest tinkering (Brooks, 1975). His machine worked for the first time in 1876 ("Mr. Watson—come here—I want to see you." [Watson, 1926, pp. 57–59]). In 1877, the Bell Telephone

---

[5]The population of New York City as estimated in the 1850 census. *Statistical Abstract of the United States* (1910).

[6]Quoted from a letter to the House of Representatives, December 17, 1844, House Executive Doc., No. 24, 28 Cong., 2 session, pp. 1–9, from (Thompson, 1947, p. 30).

Company issued its first 5,000 shares, with Bell receiving 10.[7] Similarly, David H. Houston invented the first practical roll-film camera, his 1881 Kodak. His partner, George Eastman, bought most of the patents when he formed the Eastman Dry Plate and Film Company in 1884, and by 1892, the Eastman Kodak Company owned all of the available patents.[8] A receptive American market for information and information machines encouraged imaginative Yankees to exploit each new invention for its money making potential.

As in the days of the penny press, advertising is the principal source of revenue for the modern mass media, and it encourages their proliferation, adding to the momentum of the information economy. The direct sale of information machines, products and services permeates the American economy, through complex and interdependent markets (25% of the 1967 GNP, the primary information sector, according to Porat[9]).

Moreover, the growth of these markets has also affected the distribution of labor. Part of the multiplication of information workers can be attributed to the demands of the production and distribution of information as a final product. The information marketplace requires new occupations like computer programmers and nuclear physicists, as well as older occupations like journalists and printers.

Capitalism, as an economic order, provided the incentive to convert information into a commodity. Commoditization in turn affected technology and labor. The tendency was apparent at the birth of the republic. Though it never went unopposed, the commoditization of information was clearly a vital part of American business by 1877.

Yet, capitalism alone does not fully explain the scope of all of the activities associated with the information society. Managerial systems, white-collar workers, and bureaucracies have more to do with process than with product. Regardless of their final product, these corporate structures are the result of industrialization.

Information-Oriented Industrialization

Industrialization is the path that capitalism took in the United States. Capital, machines, and labor were brought together in one place to create the industrial system (Giddens, 1973; Hacker, 1940; Heilbroner,

---

[7]It is not as bad as it appears. Mabel Hubbard received 1,497 shares and she soon married Bell (Brooks, 1975).

[8]Houston was independently wealthy and did not care to profit from his invention, to Eastman's good fortune (Hammer, 1940).

[9]"The 'primary information sector' includes those firms which supply the bundle of information goods and services exchanged in a market context" (Porat, 1977, p. 4).

1977; Heilbroner & Singer, 1984; Katz, Doucet, & Stern, 1982). Machines were introduced into the work process so extensively that eventually production could not occur without them (Hacker, 1940). With the introduction of these machines, individual workers came to be organized in a new way.[10] They became only one of many elements in the total production process. To Anthony Giddens, the transformation of human labor, via the application of inanimate sources of energy, into productive activity constitutes the essential feature of industrialism (Giddens, 1973). According to Harry Braverman, "Industrial capitalism begins when a significant number of workers is employed by a single capitalist" (Braverman, 1974, p. 59). Aspiring industrialists had to amass and expend enormous amounts of capital, for the many elements of this process to function effectively.

The United States was already a capitalist society before entrepreneurs began adapting the industrial system to the pursuit of profit. By introducing industrialism, they were acting within a social context already committed to an established economic system.

The principal advantage of the industrial system was its ability to exploit the momentum of growth. When factories increased production, the numbers of units produced went up but the cost per unit went down. These economies of scale resulted from greater productive efficiency and offered greater profit margins, as well as competitive advantage (Brownlee, 1974). Each was a powerful incentive for growth.

But the benefits of growth were not solely economic; they were also political. President Ulysses S. Grant enjoyed the company of Jay Cooke, Jim Fiske, and Jay Gould, all wealthy directors of large railroad companies. Leland Stanford, a partner in the Southern Pacific Railroad monopoly later became governor of the state of California (Josephson, 1934). Large business organizations wielded more influence with government. Their political weight could be coupled with their economic advantage to gain and protect large shares of the market (Heilbroner, 1977).

Sheer size, however, brought problems along with advantages. Huge firms that dominated their industries also suffered growing pains. Older, more personal styles of management were inappropriate to organizations where owners could not visit every factory owned by the company. Indeed, the entrepreneurs who started these businesses often did not have the personalities or skills to run complex organizations. Corporate growth created a crisis of control, whose solution was found in the development of a system of supervision (Heilbroner, 1977).

---

[10]The division of labor and its advantages had been noted in the 18th century by Adam Smith (1902) when he examined a pin factory. But it was not yet recognizable as the industrial system.

Daniel C. McCallum, a general superintendent of the New York and Erie Railroad, pioneered the system that evolved modern administrative management. He recognized that an organization's principal administrator should be the focus of both authority and communication. Moreover, the key to controlling a complex organization such as a railroad rested in the continuous flow of information from the bottom to the top. He restructured the railroad and stimulated the flow of information through hourly, daily, weekly, and monthly reports on all matters of operation. He received many of these reports by telegraph and condensed them into statistical summaries (Chandler, 1977, p. 103).

As part of the reorganization of 1855, he drew what was probably the first organization table. The chart itself is lost, but Alfred Chandler has preserved a description:

> The design of the chart was a tree whose roots represented the president and the board of directors; the branches were the five operating divisions and the service departments, engine repairs, car, bridge, telegraph, printing, and the treasurer's and the secretary's offices; while the leaves indicated the various local ticket, freight, and forwarding agents, subordinate superintendents, train crews, foremen, and so forth.[11]

McCallum's innovation of technique became the basis for administrative management and the massive corporate bureaucracies that exist today.

The adoption of administrative management required two commitments from managers. First, they needed to believe in the superiority of rational decision-making over intuitive decision-making. They could not allow themselves the excitement of wheeling and dealing in the manner of their predecessors. McCallum wrote to the president of the New York and Erie, "It is very important, however, that principal officers should be in possession of all the information necessary to enable them to judge correctly as to the industry and efficiency of subordinates of every grade" (McCallum, 1956, p. 104). Henry Varnum Poor, the influential editor of the *American Railroad Journal*, also noted this new development, "By the energies and genius of our superintendents, it [railroad management] is approaching the position of an accurate science; not limited to theoretical discussion, but developing reliable formulae for the practical estimates of the engineer" (*American Railroad Journal*, 1855, p. 568).

In contrast, Jay Gould created an enormous railroad empire by manipulating stocks and favors. But he had also been willing to risk the entire enterprise through his machinations (Heilbroner, 1977; O'Con-

---

[11]Interestingly, McCallum's picturesque illustration did not last. Within a few years, the New York and Erie had adopted the abstract form of lines and boxes familiar today (Chandler, 1956).

nor, 1962). His successors eschewed such intuitive behavior in favor of the security of systematic planning and organization. If decisions were to be made systematically, then the decision makers would need to make informed judgments. The new approach demanded more information.

Second, managers would have to develop the means to provide information to those making decisions. Rational decision making could not function without clear and easy access to whatever information managers deemed necessary. Like the New York and Erie, large firms began to sprout departments. When Alfred P. Sloan came to General Motors in 1918, he noted to his surprise that, ". . . no one knew how much was being contributed—plus or minus—by each division to the common good of the corporation" (Sloan, 1963, p. 48). Staff departments were the solution. They, and the new middle managers that came with them, introduced new forms of administration and coordination. Sloan stood at the cusp of this transition within General Motors. "Mr. Durant had been able to operate the corporation in his own way, as the saying goes, 'by the seat of his pants.' The new administration was made up of men with very different ideas about business administration. They desired a highly rational and objective mode of operation" (Sloan, 1963, p. 52).

Sloan's organization study of GM was the vehicle. He recommended broad changes, among them:

1. Determining the actual functioning of the various departments, "not only in relation to one another, but in relation to the central organization."
2. Developing statistics to determine the relation between net return and the invested capital of each operating division.
3. Centralizing the power of all executive functions in the president, as chief executive of the corporation.
4. Limiting to the practical minimum, the number of executives reporting directly to the president (Sloan, 1963).

These last two, in particular, required building an enormous infrastructure to funnel information from the distant corners of the corporation to the president through a series of progressive summaries. General Motors came to be administered by employees who were not owners but professionals. Similarly, the Gambles, Swifts, Armours, Eastmans, Bordens, Deerings, and McCormicks gradually removed themselves from operational control of the firms they had founded. They owned but no longer managed (Chandler, 1977).

Belief in rational decisionmaking, along with commitment to institutionalize it in a system of access to information, resolved the crisis of control and laid the foundation for the "technostructure" observed in all corporations of the 20th century (Galbraith, 1967). Corporations now devote a large proportion of their resources to maintaining their managerial bureaucracies, purchasing information from outside vendors, as well as from internal sources.

Organizational success achieved through the application of managerial techniques, has encouraged managers to apply the system elsewhere in the economy. Large corporations even try to manage the marketplace itself by influencing prices and encouraging specific demand for their products. Galbraith notes in *The New Industrial State* (1967):

> Although advertising will be thought the central feature of this management, and is certainly important, much more is involved. . . . The management of demand consists of devising a sales strategy for a particular product. It also consists in devising a product, around which a sales strategy can be built. Product design, model change, packaging and even performance reflect the need to provide what are called strong selling points. They are thus as much a part of the process of demand management as an advertising campaign. (p. 213)

The language of management refers to this as the "marketing mix." In order for it to be achieved, it requires the extension of the information infrastructure beyond the original demands of administrative management.

In this century, administrative management has been the dominant paradigm for decision-making, and has diffused far beyond industrial enterprises, even to interpersonal services like health care and religious organizations. It has become *the* culturally-approved way to make decisions in all organized settings, so that even if intuition is the actual basis for making a judgment, the form of administrative management is followed. Industrialization transformed American values by introducing new ways to make decisions and to accomplish goals. Information replaced intuition and tradition, as the currency for making decisions, first within the corporation and later beyond it. Indeed, even though the goals of government are different from those of the corporation, it too has modelled itself along these same lines.

McCallum, Sloan, and their fellows, responded to the powerful social forces of capitalism. Administrative management was one characteristic consequence of industrialization, and a major cause of the growth in the production and distribution of information, with its accompanying information infrastructure.

INFORMATION SOCIETY AS A TYPE OF INDUSTRIAL CAPITALISM

Morse and McCallum travelled along parallel lines. Morse took the first unwilling steps that would transform the sale of information leading to its place as a major commodity. McCallum laid the foundation for a social structure to exploit what Morse had wrought. From the 1850s, the growing demand for information to coordinate the production and distribution of all goods and services complemented the sale of information as a commodity.

If the roots of the information society are embedded in early American capitalism and industrialization, then is there evidence for continuity in the 20th century as well? If so, we would expect to find patterns of continuous growth in the available data, rather than discontinuity signalled by a precipitous increase.

Patents, trademarks, and copyrights reflect the uses of information as a commodity and represent gross measures of continuity, though it is impossible to separate the contribution of capitalism from the contribution of industrialization in the data. As the instruments by which Morse and Bell protected their ideas, patent, trademark, and copyright growth represents a turn toward the sale of information and the rise of the information economy. All three have increased dramatically in absolute numbers. But when controlled for population growth, they show no such pattern of increase.

The number of trademarks rose most rapidly between 1900 and 1930, the years when large scale consumer markets were established.

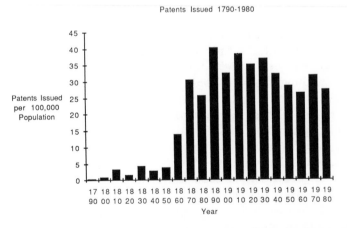

Patents Issued 1790-1980

Figure 3.1. Sources: U.S. Bureau of the Census, *Historical Statistics of the United States, Colonial Times, to 1970*, Washington DC, 1975, Tables W99, W107, W82, A2. U.S. Bureau of the Census, *Statistical Abstract of the United States: 1981*, (102nd edition). Washington DC, 1981, Tables 1, 945, 975.

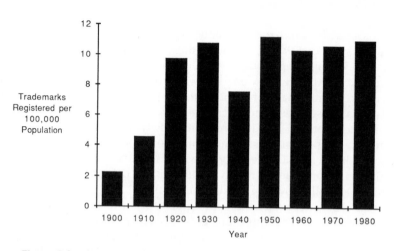

Trademarks Registered 1900-1980

Figure 3.2. Sources: U.S. Bureau of the Census, *Historical Statistics of the United States, Colonial Times, to 1970*, Washington DC, 1975, Tables W99, W107, W82, A2. U.S. Bureau of the Census, *Statistical Abstract of the United States: 1981*, (102nd edition). Washington DC, 1981, Tables 1, 945, 975.

Likewise, the greatest increases in issued patents occurred between 1850 and 1890, the years of the industrial revolution. These increases do reflect the growing importance of information as a commodity. But they are closely tied to the period of industrialization.

Growth of white-collar workers in the labor force is another good measure, especially since it reflects managerial demands and the sale of information (Machlup & Kronwinkler, 1975). We find steady growth from 1900 to 1980, with a slight dip beginning in 1930 that is made up by 1950. If anything, the period after 1970 seems to indicate a lessening in the growth of white-collar workers.[12]

Desire to control both the industrial system and market led to the present distribution of information workers, information technologies, messages, and channels. When preliminary data from the 20th century are added to the historical evidence, they support the interpretation that industrialization *and* capitalism caused the expansion of those activities collectively defined as the information society.

If we are to further understand this progression, a number of questions remain to be answered.

[12]In the United States the forces of capitalism and industrialization are virtually inseparable when examining data at the level of abstraction attempted in this article.

How does the movement toward information-orientation differ when capitalism is removed from the equation? Studying those few industrial societies which are not capitalist might provide clues as to the relative influence of industrialization. For example, a comparative analysis of the Soviet Union and the United States would further our understanding of different paths information-orientation and of the interaction between capitalism and industrialization.

How does information become a public resource and how does information become a commodity? Can we identify patterns where information that was once treated as a public resource converts to a commodity, or vice versa? Capitalism, which drives commoditization, acts amidst countervailing forces. The framing of the constitution and the development of the telegraph indicate complex phenomena. Thinking of them as a tension might provide greater understanding.

How do information occupations experience industrialization? Is the software industry repeating the history of automobile production? We have hints that white-collar jobs are susceptible to mechanization (see Downing, 1981) and that they differ in levels of susceptibility (Schement, Curtis, & Lievrouw, 1985). But imprecise categories, like white-collar worker, hinder analysis.

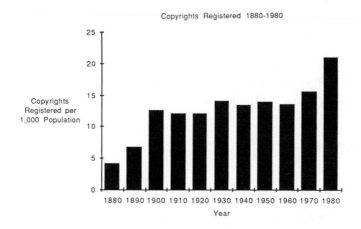

Figure 3.3. Sources: U.S. Bureau of the Census, *Historical Statistics of the United States, Colonial Times, to 1970,* Washington DC, 1975, Tables W99, W107, W82, A2. U.S. Bureau of the Census, *Statistical Abstract of the United States: 1981,* (102nd edition). Washington DC, 1981, Tables 1, 945, 975.

Table 3.1 Percentages of the White-Collar Labor Force 1910-1980

1900	1910	1920	1930	1940	1950	1960	1970	1980
17.6	21.3	24.9	29.4	31.1	36.6	46.6	50.8	53.9

Source: U.S. Bureau of the Census, *Working Paper No. 5,* "Occupational Trends in the United States, 1900-1950." U.S. Bureau of the Census, *Statistical Abstract of the United States: 1981,* (102nd edition). Washington DC, 1981, Table 672, "Occupations of Employed Workers—Percent Distribution, by Race: 1960 to 1980."

CODA

The key to understanding the information society depends on recognizing elements of both change and continuity. American industry is no longer hog butcher to the world, because it has changed, or more properly, evolved away from its earlier form. Instead, it is now educator, banker, entertainer, and data processor to the world, and for the same reasons as before—because of the profit motive and the industrial character of these activities.

It is a myth, albeit a powerful one, to view the information society as unique or historically unprecedented. Bell and others mistake the early forms of industrialization—the smokestacks and the factories—for the social system itself. Schiller and his colleagues correctly identified capitalism as a cause, but failed to push their analysis to include industrialization. Today, the United States produces and distributes information as its primary economic activity. Capitalism remains the motivator and industrialism remains the organizing principle, but with an information-orientation.

Between the ore cars and smoke stacks of Heilbroner's vision of the 19th century, and the satellites and microchips of Williams' vision of the 20th century, lie changes that transformed the United States. We are just beginning to understand them.

REFERENCES

American Railroad Journal, (Sept. 8, 1855) Vol. XXVIII p. 568.

Baran, P. A., & Sweezy, P. M. (1966). *Monopoly capital.* New York: Monthly Review Press.

Bell, D. (1973). *The coming of post-industrial society.* New York: Basic Books.

Braudel, F. (1979). *Civilization and capitalism 15th–18th century* (Vol. II The wheels of commerce). New York: Harper & Row Publishers.

Braverman, H. (1974). *Labor and monopoly capital: The degradation of work in the twentieth century.* New York: Monthly Review Press.

Brooks, J. (1975). *Telephone: The first hundred years.* New York: Harper & Row.

Brownlee, W. E. (1974). *Dynamics of ascent: A history of the American economy.* New York: Knopf.

Chandler, A. D. Jr. (1956). Henry Varnum Poor: Business editor, analyst, and reformer. Cambridge, MA: Harvard University Press.

Chandler, A. D. Jr. (1977). *The visible hand: The managerial revolution in American business.* Cambridge, MA: Harvard University Press.

Crawford, S. (1983). The origin and development of a concept: The information society. *Bulletin of the Medical Library Association,* 71(4) 380–385.

Department of Commerce/Patent & Trademark Office. (July, 1981). *The story of the United States Patent and Trademark Office.* Washington DC: U.S. Government Printing Office.

Dizard, W. P. Jr. (1982). *The coming information age: An overview of technology, economics, and politics.* New York: Longman.

Douglas, S., & Guback, T. (July, 1984). Production and technology in the communication/information revolution. *Media, Culture and Society.* 6 233–245.

Downing, H. (1981). Word processors and the oppression of women. In T. Forestor (Ed.), *The microelectronics revolution* (pp. 275–287). Cambridge, MA: MIT Press.

Drucker, P. (1969). *The age of discontinuity,* New York: Harper & Row.

Eisenhower, D. D. (1971). Farewell radio and television address to the American people, January 17, 1961. In J. R. Wish & S. H. Gamble (Eds.), *Marketing and social issues* (pp. 175–177). New York: John Wiley & Sons.

Forestor, T. (Ed.). (1981). *The microelectronics revolution.* Cambridge, MA: MIT Press.

Galbraith, J. K. (1967). *The new industrial state.* New York: The New American Library.

Giddens, A. (1973). *The class structure of advanced societies.* New York: Hutchinson, Anchor Press.

Hacker, L. M. (1940). *The triumph of American capitalism.* New York: Simon and Schuster.

Hammer, D. P. (1976). *The information age: Its development and impact.* Metuchen, NJ: Scarecrow Press.

Hammer, M. F. (1940). *History of the Kodak and its continuations: The first folding and panoramic cameras.* Walla Walla, WA: Pioneer Publications.

Harrington, M. (1977). Post-industrial society and the welfare state. In L. Estabrook (Ed.), *Libraries in post-industrial society* (pp. 19–29). Phoenix, AZ: Oryx Press.

Heilbroner, R. L. (1973). Economic problems of a 'post-industrial' society. *Dissent,* 20(2), 163–176.

Heilbroner, R. L. (1977). *The economic transformation of America.* New York: Harcourt Brace Jovanovich.

Heilbroner, R. L. & Singer, A. (1984). *The economic transformation of America: 1600 to the present.* (2nd ed.). New York: Harcourt Brace Jovanovich.

Josephson, M. (1934). *The robber barons: The great American industrialists 1861–1901.* New York: Harcourt Brace Jovanovich.

Julien, P. A., Lamonde, P., & Latouche, D. (1976). Post-industrial society: Vague and dangerous concept. *Futuribles,* 7, 309–320.

Katz, M. B., Doucet, M. J., & Stern, M. J. (1982). *The social organizations of early industrial capitalism.* Cambridge, MA: Harvard University Press.

Machlup, F. (1958). *An economic review of the patent system* (Study of the Subcommittee on Patents, Trademarks, and Copyrights, of the Committee on the Judiciary, Study No. 15). Washington, DC: GPO.

Machlup, F. (1962). *The production and distribution of knowledge in the United States,* Princeton, NJ: Princeton University Press.

Machlup, F. & Kronwinkler, T. (1975). Workers who produce knowledge: A steady increase, 1900 to 1970. *Weltwirtschaftliches Archiv,* 111(4), 752–759.

McCallum, D. C. (1956). Superintendent's report, March 25, 1856. *Annual Report of the New York and Erie Railroad Company for 1855* (p. 39) In A. D. Chandler, Jr. (Ed.), *Railroads the nation's first big business: Sources and readings.* (p. 104). New York: Harcourt Brace & World.

Meehan, E. R. (1984, 6 July). Towards a third vision of an information society. *Media, Culture and Society,* 257–271.

Mosco, V. (1982). *Push button fantasies.* Norwood, NJ: Ablex.

Nora, S. & Minc, A. (1980). *The computerization of society: A report to the president of France,* Cambridge, MA: MIT Press.

Ochai, A. (1984). The emerging information society. *International Library Review,* 16(4), 367–372.

O'Connor, R. (1962). *Gould's millions.* New York: Doubleday.

Porat, M. U. (1977). *The information economy: Definition and measurement.* (OT Special Publication 77-12[1]). Washington, DC: U.S. Department of Commerce.

Price, D. J. de S. (1963). *Little science big science.* New York: Columbia University Press.

Rostow, W. W. (Ed.). (1963). *The economics of take-off into sustained growth.* New York: St. Martin's Press.

Rostow, W. W. (1971). *The stages of economic growth* (2nd ed.). Cambridge, UK: Cambridge University Press.

Rostow, W. W. (1978). *The world economy: History & prospect.* Austin, TX: University of Texas Press.

Schement, J. R. & Lievrouw, L. A. (1984, Dec.). A behavioural measure of information work. *Telecommunications Policy,* 321–334.

Schement, J. R., Parker, J., & Shelton, C. (1985). *A bibliography of the information society.* Report of the Graduate School of Library and Information Science, University of California, Los Angeles.

Schement, J. R., Curtis, T., & Lievrouw, L. A. (1985). Social factors affecting the success of introducing information technology into the workplace. *Proceedings of the 48th ASIS Annual Meeting* (pp. 278–283) White Plains, NY: Knowledge Industry Publications Inc.

Schiller, D. (1981). *Objectivity and the news: The public and the rise of commercial journalism.* Philadelphia, PA: University of Pennsylvania Press.

Schiller, H. I. (1981). *Who knows: Information in the age of the Fortune 500,* Norwood, NJ: Ablex.

Schudson, M. (1984). *The uneasy persuasion.* New York: Basic Books.

Slack, J. Daryl. (1984, July 6). The information revolution as ideology. *Media, Culture and Society,* 247.

Sloan, A. P. Jr. (1963). *My years with General Motors.* New York: Doubleday.

Smith, A. (1902). *An inquiry into the nature and causes of the wealth of nations.* New York: American Dome Library Co.

Ssewczyk, J. (1970). Totalna aliencja i prymtiywny hedonizm: Kapitalizm ery postindustrialnej (Total alienation and primitive hedonism: The post-industrial era capitalism). *Studian Filozoficzne,* 1, 171–188.

U.S. Bureau of the Census. (1910). *Statistical Abstract of the United States.* Government Printing Office.

Stearns, P. N. (Summer 1984). The idea of post-industrial society: Some problems. *Journal of Social History,* 17, 685–694.

Thompson, R. L. (1947). *Wiring a continent: The history of the telegraph industry in the United States 1832–1866.* Princeton, NJ: Princeton University Press.

Toffler, A. (1980). *The third wave.* New York: Bantam.

Watson, T. A. (1926). *Exploring life: The autobiography of Thomas A. Watson,* New York: D. Appleton.

Williams, F. (1982). *The communication revolution.* Beverly Hills, CA: Sage.

4 Silicon Valley: A Scenario for the Information Society of Tomorrow

JUDITH K. LARSEN
DataQuest

EVERETT M. ROGERS
University of Southern California

Technology is creating a society in which information forms the basic resource. The post-industrial, or information society, is a society in which information technology supports manufacturing and administration. Although tool technology is an extension of the individual's physical powers, information technology is an extension of perception and knowledge, and thus enlarges our consciousness. In this sense, information technology is basic to all other technologies.

The transition from an industrial society to an information society is accompanied by widespread social and individual change. Nowhere is this change more advanced than in Silicon Valley, America's high-tech heartland. Like the technological innovations developed in Silicon Valley and then flowing to the rest of the world, social patterns now evolving in Silicon Valley may be precursors of the future for other communities.

As the information society spreads and replaces the industrial society, social and cultural characteristics of the new society also emerge. A consequence of this change is the rapid breakdown of traditional patterns and supports of the old society, a change often causing problems for social systems and for people as they try to define new models and to superimpose them on existing patterns. The lifestyle changes occurring in the information society may be as critical and as difficult as the earlier transition from an agricultural to an industrial society. What is clear is that we are moving into a different way of life but without a full understanding of its characteristics or consequences.

SILICON VALLEY TODAY

Just as Manchester and the Saar Valley and Pittsburgh were once the centers of an industrial society, today's information society has a heartland—Silicon Valley. Silicon Valley is located in a 30-by-10-mile strip between San Jose and San Francisco. Almost all of Silicon Valley lies in Santa Clara County, California, which in 1950 was the prune capital of America. The county had only 800 manufacturing employees then, and half of them worked in canneries and food processing plants. The fruit trees have all but disappeared, replaced by semiconductors, computers, and other microelectronics firms.

Today Silicon Valley is the nation's ninth largest manufacturing center, with sales of over $40 billion annually. The electronics industry on which the information society is based presently accounts for some $100 billion in annual sales. By the end of this decade, electronics will reach annual sales of $400 billion and become the world's fourth largest industry after steel, autos, and chemicals. Electronics, the basic source of information technology, is the largest employer in Silicon Valley, providing 162,000 jobs in 1983 (Bank of America, 1983). About 40,000 new jobs are created in the Valley each year. Its economy is the fastest growing and wealthiest in the United States with a median family income of over $26,000 according to the U.S. Census.

Specifically, it is the semiconductor industry that earns Silicon Valley the title of America's high-tech heartland. Semiconductors, popularly called "chips," are the basic component in virtually all microelectronics products; therefore, the semiconductor industry can be considered the basic technology-producing industry. Of the approximately 150 semiconductor companies in the United States, all but a handful are centered in Silicon Valley.

Naturally, semiconductor users are attracted to locate close to semiconductor suppliers, and as a result, other microelectronic industries have congregated in Silicon Valley. Computers, one of the largest users of semiconductors, are a major Silicon Valley industry, along with computer peripherals, instrumentation, and software.

Silicon Valley includes a large population of information workers, people whose work mainly involves processing information. Scholars studying the information society (Machlup, 1962; Porat, 1978) assign the majority of people in the information society to this category. The information society is based on a relatively small number of information technology producers, who are included as information workers. They make the tools (like computers) for other information workers to use.

Unlike most other communities, a large proportion of the Silicon Valley workforce consists of people who produce information technology. Individuals employed in Silicon Valley's microelectronics industries produce the tools that enable knowledge workers to perform their jobs. Information technology producers are particularly basic to the information society.

In 1985 the semiconductor industry struggled through its worst year in history with the result that employment was severely affected in Silicon Valley. Nearly all semiconductor companies reduced employment levels either through layoffs or attrition. Worldwide employment in the semiconductor industry was down an estimated 14% in 1985, resulting in the elimination of 60,000 jobs (Dataquest, 1985). Companies in the semiconductor equipment and materials industry did not cut employment as soon as semiconductor manufacturers, yet the same pattern of layoffs appeared with a time lag of one or two months (Grenier, 1985). Similar patterns are apparent in industries whose products are heavy users of semiconductors, such as computers. The 1985 slump in Silicon Valley illustrates the up-and-down nature of the microelectronics industry.

ENTREPRENEURISM

Entrepreneurial Silicon Valley represents the work ethic of the information society in the extreme: fast pace, long hours, and a high commitment to work. The workaholics who want job success and big money are bright, and they devote their disciplined minds to very hard work. Virtually everyone, from line-operators (skilled manual workers on semiconductor assembly lines) to executives, complain about the fast pace, intensity, and stress of the microelectronics industry. Yet these individuals acknowledge that the long hours are dictated by the need to be first to market with a new product, to be technologically competitive. New information technologies on the cutting edge of development may be truly unique, but are usually so for only a few months, until a competitor brings out a newer and better version of the technology. The fast pace suggests that one's job success depends on speed—and often it does.

Many social observers state that the transformation of the United States and other industrialized nations into information societies is caused, at least in part, by new information technologies, especially by semiconductors and by computers. Although information technology is crucial, an equally important component in the current social transition is entrepreneurial spirit. Entrepreneurism and information technology, two critical factors in today's social change, are complexly interrelated. Silicon Valley is the world center for microelectronic innovation; Silicon Valley also extols the entrepreneurial spirit and its associated work ethic, lifestyle, and social values. Technological innovation and entrepreneurship together support today's emerging information society.

Silicon Valley's information society represents a trend from organization man to entrepreneur. A spurt of entrepreneurial activity has occurred in recent years. In 1950, 93,000 new companies opened their doors in the United States; in the 1980s, there are nearly 600,000 start-ups annually. Many of the new start-ups are in the microelectronics industry; a fair number are spin-offs of older, established companies.

Silicon Valley has produced an amazing number of new electronics firms. Companies are constantly starting up, growing, merging, being acquired, or fading away, making it difficult to know exactly how many firms exist at any one time. A recent count (Schmieder, 1983) identified 2,736 microelectronics *manufacturing* firms in Silicon Valley. In addition to manufacturing companies, Silicon Valley includes many companies supporting the microelectronics manufacturers: Companies engaged in marketing, advertising, research and development, consulting, training, and providing venture capital, legal, and other support services. There are at least as many of these companies as manufacturers, so the total number of firms in the electronics industry in Silicon Valley is probably at least 6,000—and still growing.

In addition to the surprising number of microelectronics firms, another startling fact is their small size. Over two-thirds of the microelectronics manufacturing firms in Silicon Valley have from one to ten employees and 85% have fewer than 50 staff members. Media attention is concentrated on the 54 electronics firms with more than 1,000 employees, firms such as Hewlett-Packard, Intel, and Apple Computer. These giants constitute only 2% of the electronics companies in Silicon Valley, although they represent half or more of the total workforce in microelectronics manufacturing.

KEY FACTORS IN ENTREPRENEURISM

Several factors are characteristic of entrepreneurism in Silicon Valley and they are necessary for the successful development of other high-technology heartlands in the United States and overseas (Rogers & Larsen, 1984).

Availability of skilled technical people. More than any other single factor, Silicon Valley high-tech companies depend on individuals who can design cleanrooms, tool delicate features, and design innovative products. This priceless human resource is placated and wooed. Few other places in the world can offer the pool of experienced, specialized high-tech brainpower. Companies that want access to this expertise have little choice but to locate where these intellectual resources are concentrated.

Infrastructure. Sunnyvale, a city in the center of Silicon Valley, is the only community in the world with miles of hydrogen mains under its city streets, along with water and sewer lines. Cleanrooms, the daily delivery of liquid gas, and local machine shops with tolerance measured in microns, are part of the infrastructure of the microelectronics industry. Hundreds of specialized services support this industry: transportation vans for computers and other delicate equipment, venture capitalists who understand high-technology financing, advertising and public relations firms that can tell Winchesters from floppies, and lawyers specializing in bringing companies public.

Venture capital. Silicon Valley is a prime center of venture capital activity. Over one-third of the nation's largest venture capital companies have an office located in or near Silicon Valley. Many of the remaining venture capital firms, though based elsewhere, have heavily invested in Silicon Valley firms. In 1983, over $5.8 billion were at work in United States venture capital investments. Venture capital provides the start-up funds for microelectronics companies that have no financial collateral other than a hot technological idea for a new product.

Job mobility. The annual rate of job turnover in Silicon Valley is about 30% among professionals (Murray, 1981). The average professional has three different jobs each ten years. Such high turnover is encouraged by the shortage of qualified, experienced personnel. Thus, companies are oriented toward the near-term, offering benefits and incentives to their employees that are attractive now, such as stock options, recreational facilities, and extensive training programs. High job mobility is a boon or a disaster, depending on one's perspective. For employees, the assurance of being able to leave one company and move easily to another with an increase in salary provides a kind of ultimate social security. Understandably, companies have quite a different view of job-hopping. For them, the loss of experienced employees is a major problem. The constant turnover among their staff creates difficulties in establishing internal operating networks. If a key engineer on a design project leaves a firm, much of the information behind the project also goes.

The most common incentive for job-hopping is more money; a move to a new job usually represents a raise of at least 15%. For the company, problems caused by the shortage of technical people means that paying more is sometimes the only way to attract needed personnel.

Job-hopping is also a way of advancing a career through a series of moves up the corporate ladder. Paradoxically, in Silicon Valley job-hopping provides greater opportunity for advancement than staying with one company. By job-hopping, the employee moves to a more respectable position with more pay. In contrast, there is less chance of being promoted by loyalty to one company.

Information-exchange networks. Everyone knows everyone in Silicon Valley due to the high rate of job mobility and the concentrated geographical location of the industry. The extensive network of personal contacts facilitates information exchange. A Federal Trade Commission report states that the unique strength of the U.S. semiconductor industry derives from its firms' rapid copying of each others' technological innovations.

Information-exchange is the predominant function of these interpersonal networks, and there are widely-held norms for what constitutes an ethical information-exchange. According to the Semiconductor Industry Association (Davis, 1981), "Information-exchange is fine under ethical conditions but not under non-ethical." The definitions of these terms are unwritten but well known to individuals in the Silicon Valley information society:

> It is ethical if you leave a company and take your ideas and plans with you. In this way, spin-offs occur and are considered ethical. However, it is unethical if another company identifies someone who might have the information they want, and they come in and steal that person. That creates hard feelings all the way around. (Davis, personal communication, 1981)

A primary norm of information exchange is reciprocity. It is acceptable for an individual to give technical information to another person, as long as the first person expects to receive information in return. It is not considered acceptable to provide information when there is no expectation of reciprocity; then the individual is considered an informer, and thus as untrustworthy.

Another norm concerns personal relationships. Personal networks thrive in Silicon Valley's advanced information society, and even in such a cut-throat industry as microelectronics, warm personal relationships exist. It is generally acceptable for information technology producers to exchange certain technical information with a colleague working for another firm if such information-exchange is based on close personal ties. However, it is not considered ethical to share corporate proprietary information, regardless of the strength of personal ties.

There is a point at which information-exchange must stop, both for the firm and for the individual. Most professionals have a good idea of where this thin line is, and most observe it. Individuals in Silicon Valley are wary of information requests coming from competitors, and will provide information to competitors only if it is "behind the times." They will not exchange information on current processes or activities that might hurt their present employer.

Local role models. Spin-offs from established firms are common in Silicon Valley. Technology is expanding so rapidly that no one company can possibly develop all potential innovations. This climate encourages spin-offs, and many are successful. It is believed that almost anyone can form a new company: "If he can start a new company, why can't I?" As the entrepreneurial spirit spreads and gains support in Silicon Valley, the technological innovation and social change that accompanies it also gains wide acceptance.

THE TOLL EXACTED BY SILICON VALLEY

In the extremely competitive work environment of Silicon Valley's information society, the fast pace and long hours take their toll on personal life and families. Human relationships are strained, with the results affecting not only employees but spouse and family as well. In 1980, Santa Clara County reported 10,900 divorces, more than the number of marriages (*San Jose Mercury*, 1981). This divorce rate is higher than the rate for California as a whole, and California's rate is 20% above the U.S. average.

Silicon Valley family life is in the midst of change. According to the 1980 census, one of five families with children under 18 was headed by a single parent. Women headed slightly more than one in every ten households (Watson, 1982). As a result of the high divorce rate, there is a large number of single parent households, mostly headed by women. Many work in Silicon Valley microelectronic firms.

The Silicon Valley work ethic may be the wave of the future. Perhaps it is functional in an information society where technology prevails and individual competence is rewarded. Nevertheless, if this ethic becomes the model for the emerging information society, serious social problems with far-reaching implications will accompany it.

Although Silicon Valley may be the "permanent" location for most information technology producers, their immediate living arrangements are often transient. According to a recent study of Silicon Valley employees (Larsen & Gill, 1984), nearly half of the respondents had lived in their present location less than five years. This rate of housing turnover was reported by people at all age levels; therefore, it appears that living arrangements for many people in Silicon Valley do not stabilize with age, but continue to change and evolve over a lifetime.

The range of household configurations is also broad. The "traditional" American household—mother, father, and two children—is characteristic of less than half of Silicon Valley residents (Larsen, 1984). Other household arrangements commonly reported include self and children, self and spouse with no children, and self living with related and nonrelated persons. Half of Silicon Valley individuals report that their household experienced change within the past two years. One-third report that they expected their present household to remain as it was no more than six months.

Time pressures of working in entrepreneurial Silicon Valley directly affect families and children. About half of the mothers in our 1984 study and three-fourths of the fathers spent less than 2 hours a day with their children, yet nearly half of the respondents were satisfied with that time arrangement. Those who were not satisfied regretted that there was not more time to spend with their children.

Like their parents, Silicon Valley children's lives are very full; one-third of the mothers reported that their children had little free time available outside of school, so the children's flexibility for participating in family activities also was limited. About one-fourth of the families were able to get together as a group on holidays or other such occasions; however, about half of the families did things together as a group once a week.

The high rate of change in personal living arrangements and the lack of time for families to spend together contributes to the sense of instability frequently described as characterizing the emerging information society. For many members of the emerging society, their personal living situation fails to provide a dependable working base.

WORKING IN THE INFORMATION SOCIETY

Work is a central component in the lives of many information technology producers in Silicon Valley. One-third of our respondents reported that for them, work was a basic requirement for their overall well-being: "Work is completely central to me. It is the most important thing I do." For another one-third, work was important but not predominant. These people described themselves as career oriented, but thought there was more to life than just work. The remaining one-third said they thought about work only from 8:00 to 5:00. They perceived work as an economic necessity, not as a primary aspect of their life.

If dedication to work can be measured by hours worked per week, those participating in the Silicon Valley information society constitute a very dedicated group. Over 63% of the respondents reported working more than 40 hours per week. Indeed, many people at higher job levels observed that there was a "peer culture" of working extra hours, and that they felt guilty if they went home "on time" rather than staying late. The dedication required by Silicon Valley's work ethic demands that people work long hours and relinquish their personal concerns for professional success. Our respondents also were asked for their observations of the place of work in the information society. Nearly two-thirds thought that people in Silicon Valley's information society were more work-oriented than elsewhere, a statement consistent with their assertion that for them, work is very central in their lives.

QUALITY OF LIFE

People comprising Silicon Valley's information society have given considerable thought to the emerging society and related issues regarding the quality of life; discussion of such topics is common. In general, Silicon Valley residents think that the positive elements of the information society outweigh the negative aspects. As a Silicon Valley resident told us: "There is excitement in being part of a revolution. You watch it grow and change, and you realize you're at the vanguard of what everyone is going to experience." Most people thought the opportunity for jobs provided by the information society was its greatest asset, followed closely by the exciting nature of the work, educational programs, recreational and cultural activities, and by the belief that they were making a substantial contribution to the microelectronics industry and to an emerging form of society.

What is the impact of the emerging information society on the attitudes and values of its people? Most individuals believe that interpersonal values in Silicon Valley are different from the society in which they grew up. Specifically, they state that life in Silicon Valley is more competitive, more career-oriented, faster, and places greater emphasis on the individual than on family and community. Further, they feel sexual mores are more permissive, and that there is a more tolerant attitude toward different kinds of people. Indeed, most people feel that "traditional" values of home, family, and community do not apply in the Silicon Valley information society.

Traditionally, the institutions of church, school, and public government have been viewed as the foundations of society by most Americans. Virtually every individual and family has come in contact with these institutions and has been affected by them. However, these traditional institutions are not very central to life in Silicon Valley. Most people have little or no interest in church-related activities or in community or civic activities. Individuals reported a good deal of interest in school-related activities of their children. But although most parents expressed interest in their children's school activities, they had little involvement in them. This apparent paradox is explained by the time constraints faced by working parents. They experienced long, concentrated work days and by night they are too tired to participate in school activities.

The negative aspects of Silicon Valley's information society are part of its reality. The disregard for established institutions and the lack of traditional values is a problem to many.

> Traditional values place the center of life in the home, family and community. That's not the way it is here. People focus on themselves, or on one significant person—that's all. There's a withdrawal of concern for others. I don't know where I fit into this. I still think it's good to have those old values, but they aren't part of the way I'm living now.

Many Silicon Valley observers note that the information society overwhelms all other societal forms. As one of our respondents remarked: "Everyone here works in electronics. So when you meet people who work in other industries, you don't know what to talk about." The industry producing new information technologies is both a benevolent supplier of jobs and a tempter. "It is easy to get so caught up that you lose perspective." Most people want to rid themselves of work-related concerns when they deal with their family and friends, but many have trouble backing off. The fast pace of life, stress, and dilemma of having to choose between work and personal life pervade the society.

SUMMARY

Silicon Valley represents a special kind of advanced information society based on technology, continuous innovation, vigorous economic competition, and entrepreneurship. Understandably, the entrepreneurs of Silicon Valley take extreme pride in the system they have created. Technology has rewarded them personally, spawning millionaires at a remarkable rate. It also has contributed new jobs and tax dollars to the local area. As the cornerstone of the information society, high-tech industry has been good for the nation, providing one of the economic bright spots in a rather dreary picture of smokestack industries and displaced workers. Given these achievements, it is understandable that high-tech entrepreneurs survey their efforts with pride.

What about the future? Can and should such a record continue? Presently there is a paradox of troublesome changes in social and personal life, along with the challenges and rewards of work life in Silicon Valley. The information society emerging in Silicon Valley presents an inconsistent reality for its people. Challenges and opportunities exist as well as stresses and traps. Many people who are part of this society are aware of the rapid social changes occurring around them, and wonder about the impact of this emerging social environment on themselves and their families.

Work is a central component in the lives of most people in Silicon Valley's information society; many state that work is essential to their overall well-being. Meritocracy is the positive side of the Silicon Valley work ethic: The single most important criterion determining success is work performance. But there is also a sinister side to the work ethic: One is left with few resources and little self-esteem when one's job is taken away.

A troubling characteristic of the emerging information society is the absence of stability. Information technology producers experience a high rate of job mobility, most having been at their present job only two to three years. To exacerbate the situation, there is a high rate of change in personal living situations as well. Traditionally, people have depended on jobs and on families or households to provide support, but many of the Silicon Valley technology producers can depend on neither. For many individuals, change is pervasive, continual, and unsettling.

Families in Silicon Valley's information society are changing. The traditional nuclear family is less common than it once was. New family forms are emerging, often without intention or planning. The large number of families headed by single parents face special problems. Single parents are usually working parents, and as such have special problems with managing time. High-tech industry demands commitment and long hours from its employees, and doesn't stop to ask whether those employees also face responsibilities. Time thus becomes the enemy for these families.

For the microelectronics industry, the rate of job growth must level off as the geographical and resource limitations of Silicon Valley are reached. Already, most new electronics manufacturing jobs are being located elsewhere in the United States. But as yet there are no signs that Silicon Valley's entrepreneurial spirit is slackening. Technical expertise and entrepreneurial spirit are firmly established in Silicon Valley and to a far more pervasive degree than elsewhere in the country. Silicon Valley is still the heartland of the information society. The network, the human chain of vital information, is still working.

In the information society, information and innovation combine to produce economic value. Information is the society's chief resource. It is inexhaustible. Entrepreneurship is the information society's driving force, and it is moving with deep strength and conviction. The entrepreneurial spirit and sense of technological innovation that characterized the growth of the microelectronics industry are very much alive in its people today. If the workaholic single-mindedness of purpose can be melded with the desire for a fuller quality of life, the emerging information society may be as socially significant as the technology that spawned it.

REFERENCES

Bank of America. (1983). *Regional perspectives: Santa Clara County: 1983 outlook.* San Francisco, CA: Bank of America.

Dataquest. (1985). Semiconductor industry: Layoff update., Nov. 1. San Jose, CA: Dataquest.

Davis, W. (1981). Personal communication at the Semiconductor Industry Association, Cupertino, CA.

Grenier, J. (1985). Hard times hit the environment and materials industry. *Solid State Technology.* Sept., 79–80.

Larsen, J. K. (1984). Workaholism in the valley. *Business Woman, 3*(6), pp. 1–15.

Larsen, J. K., & Gill, C. (1984). *Changing lifestyles in silicon valley.* Los Altos, CA: Cognos Associates.

Machlup, F. (1962). *The production and distribution of knowledge in the United States.* Princeton, NJ: Princeton University Press.

Murray, T. J. (1981). Silicon valley faces up to the 'people' crunch. *Dun's Review, 16,* 60–62.

Porat, M. (1978). Global implications of the information society. *Journal of Communication, 28,* 70–79.

Rogers, E. M., & Larsen, J. K. (1984). *Silicon Valley fever.* New York: Basic Books.

Schmieder, R. (1983). *Rich's complete guide to the Silicon Valley.* Palo Alto, CA: Rich's Enterprises.

Watson, A. (1982, Oct. 1). Census data portrait of typical San Josean. *San Jose News,* pp. 1–19.

5 A Comparative Perspective on Information Societies

WILLIAM H. DUTTON
Annenberg School of Communications
University of Southern California

JAY G. BLUMLER
University of Leeds and University of Maryland

INTRODUCTION

The literature on the information society underscores the nearly universal nature of the implications flowing from technological change. In the field of communications, the changes brought on by the convergence of computing and telecommunications are said to be reshaping the ways in which families will be entertained and informed, how organizations will be structured and managed, the amount and paths that people will travel, how people will obtain services, how they will work, and the ways people will participate in the governmental process (Dutton, Blumler, & Kraemer, 1987). Most often, these implications are expected to result from certain features of the new information technologies applied to communications, such as their interactivity (Martin, 1974; Rogers, 1986).[1]

In many respects, however, the prospects posed by technological change are not universal. They vary across nations that develop, implement, govern, and use the new technologies in different ways. Compared to other nations, the most advanced consumer-oriented nations—those most closely approaching images of an information society—are in a better position to develop and apply the new media

---

[1]Information technology is defined broadly to include the people, equipment, and techniques involved with computing, telecommunications, and management science (Whisler, 1967).

and, therefore, face different opportunities and problems. But even among the most developed nations, there are national variations in responses to technological change in communications that are likely to have important social consequences. If this is the case, then a comparative perspective could prove useful to identifying national responses, the factors shaping them, and their social implications.

Therefore, this chapter offers a more explicitly comparative perspective on the study of technological change than is common to the study of communications. It presents a conceptual framework for approaching cross-national research, and applies it to a discussion of cross-national differences in the development of new cable and telecommunications systems. In this area, it identifies several categories of factors that appear central to explaining cross-national differences, illustrating each category by selected comparisons of Britain, France, West Germany, Japan, and the United States.[2]

A FRAMEWORK FOR COMPARATIVE INQUIRY

A comparative perspective is common to the communications field (Dutton, Blumler, & Kraemer, 1987; Edelstein, Bowes, & Harsel, 1978; Homet, 1979; McQuail & Siune, 1986; Rogers & Balle, 1985). However, most frameworks for comparative research in communications have focused on the mass media, particularly the press, radio, and television. These do not apply well to the comparative study of the new media (Ferguson, 1986; Rogers & Balle, 1985).

When the new media are discussed from a comparative perspective, national differences in communications are often characterized along two dimensions of variation in control over the communications industry (Homet, 1979). Some nations like the United States are said to gravitate towards more private control, whereas others like France tend towards more public control over the provision of communication infrastructures and services. Nationally unique legal-institutional arrangement like the U.S. Federal Communications Commission (FCC) form another common basis for comparison. These differences are important. However, there may be additional factors that shape cross-national differences in the development, use and impact of communications technology.

Figure 5.1 outlines a preliminary framework for the comparative study of new media. This framework is based on the hypothesis that the social

---

[2]These nations were chosen because they form the basis of an on-going study of new cable and telecommunication policy being conducted by the authors. For a more comprehensive overview of policy development in these nations, see Dutton, Blumler, and Kraemer (1987).

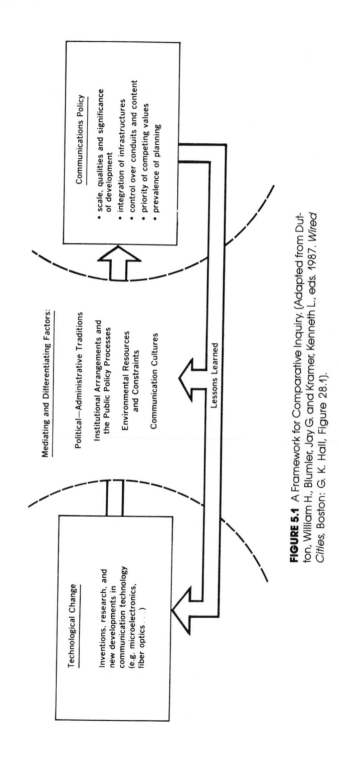

FIGURE 5.1 A Framework for Comparative Inquiry. (Adapted from Dutton, William H., Blumler, Jay G. and Kramer, Kenneth L., eds. 1987. *Wired Cities*, Boston: G. K. Hall, Figure 28.1).

implications of communication technology are shaped by both universal and particular forces, which we have distinguished within three broad categories.

The first is *technological change*, which refers to inventions, research, and developments in science and engineering that have applicability to the efficiency of communications media. As noted above, technological breakthroughs such as microelectronics present nearly universal prospects for those societies with the capacity to develop and apply them. The social implications of information and communications technology are often portrayed to be universal in that these outcomes extend from certain features of the new media (Martin, 1974; Rogers, 1986). For example, the new computer-based technologies are more interactive and provide technical facilities for two-way as well as one-way modes of electronic communication. Also, the application of information technology is almost universally viewed as leading-towards:

1. an increased number and range of communication devices that householders and businesses may obtain and use,
2. an increased number of pre-offered channels of communication material,
3. increased stores of data that users may tap into for personal and business purposes,
4. communication material more readily available at times of users' choosing,
5. and in some circumstances, individualized communication choice and reception (as distinct from the provision of wares designed for mass consumption).

Other universal implications of information technology extend from the increasingly central role that information and communication technology is expected to play in industrial and economic development, captured by scenarios of an emerging "information economy" (Porat, 1978). In this respect, the new information technologies are almost universally recognized as an opportunity for enhancing international trade and economic development (Mackintosh, 1986). The development of new telecommunication services and networks supports the expansion of the telecommunications industry, which in nearly all developed nations is being threatened with slower rates of growth as telephone penetration peaks (Dutton, Blumler, & Kraemer, 1987). They also represent business opportunities for new actors to provide equipment and services and enter areas to which they were previously excluded (Greenberger, 1985; Rogers & Larson, 1984).

Thus, one needs not be a strict technological determinist to view technological change as a major driving force behind new communications infrastructures and services that will have a variety of impacts on society. At the same time, science and technology are social constructions (Dutton & Kraemer, 1985; Woolgar, 1985). Modern communication technologies are "complex systems of people and equipment guided by technique and designed by specialists" (Danziger, Dutton, Kling, & Kraemer, 1982). Their meaning and potential application is interpreted by scientists and engineers and by society in general. In this respect, how nations receive and interpret technological developments and their impact can act as a differentiating force.[3] Thus the framework indicates that technological change is not only shaping social change, but is also subject to the influence of its social setting.

The second category is what we have called the *national setting*. This encompasses a variety of factors that mediate and differentiate national responses to technological change, including the organized interests in support or opposition to technological change, institutional arrangements governing communications, environmental resources and constraints, and the nation's communications culture (i.e., habits, beliefs, attitudes and values surrounding communications).

A third category is *national policy*, which we define from a behavioral and normative as well as a legal perspective. Communications policy is how nations and localities actually control and provide communication infrastructures and services. Communications law and regulations are important components of policy, but so are actual patterns of adoption, development, and implementation of communication infrastructures and services. In communications, as in other areas, the ways in which policies are eventually implemented can differ significantly from any abstract definition of national policy (Pressman & Wildavsky, 1973).

The major category of dependent variables in the framework is labelled *social implications*. The figure emphasizes that the social role of communications technology is shaped both by technological change and by the way nations respond to the new technology. Notwithstand-

---

[3]In Europe, changes in information technology wrought by the microelectronics revolution were not so quickly, uniformly, or unequivocally recognized as critical to industrial and economic development as they were in Japan, for example (Mackintosh, 1986, pp. 70–71). Even within nations, perceptions of technological change can vary widely. The British debate over cable policy was largely a debate over competing images of cable technology. Cable was variously perceived as a strategic resource for development of information technology; a new medium that would compete with over-the-air broadcasting; an infrastructure of a wired society; a parasite that would feed off existing mass media; or a Trojan horse that would usher in foreign programming and entrepreneurs (Dutton, 1987). Similarly, the debate over cable policy in the U.S. was tied to competing images of the nature and significance of cable technology (Dutton, Dordick, & Phillips, 1984). Who held what image influenced the outcome of the public policy process.

ing the universality of advances in communications technologies and the prospects they pose, there are likely to be important cross-national differences in how the new media are implemented and used that will shape their eventual implications for society. The arrows in Figure 5.1 indicate influences in both directions, acknowledging that the real and perceived social implications of communications have consequences for the development of new technology and policy.[4] The remaining sections elaborate this framework by discussing aspects of the national setting and national policy that shape the social role of the new media. We draw extensively from case studies of new cable and telecommunications projects. But because comparative studies of the new media are rare, many of our comparative generalizations are speculative. Our intention is to suggest themes and patterns that illustrate the value of a comparative perspective and provide some preliminary guides to empirical research.

THE NATIONAL SETTING

Four aspects of the national setting may interact with changes in information technology to mediate and differentiate national responses. These factors are:

1. the strength and interplay of organized interests, that is, the party and interest group politics of communications policy,
2. legal-institutional arrangements, including political-administrative traditions of nations that are deeply rooted and that often span beyond the communications arena to other areas of national politics and administration,
3. environmental resources and constraints relevant to communications industries and services such as the size and wealth of the domestic market,

[4]In the United States, the perceived market failures of interactive cable (e.g., the scaling down of the Qube system by Warner-Amex in 1984) and videotext systems (e.g., the Times-Mirror decision to abandon its Gateway service in 1986) have had major impacts on decisions in the private and public sectors. Similarly, in Japan, the success of major home electronics manufacturers in the American marketplace has fueled interest in the export of other forms of information technology. Internationally, the perception of some actors in major nations of Western Europe and East Asia that the United States moves toward deregulation of telecommunications and broadcasting have been a success has had repercussions on the politics of communication policy in these nations. More generally, the lessons learned from past ventures are an important part of a nation's socialization regarding what information technology and industries can and cannot do. These lessons are learned and absorbed and repeated by policy elites. In these ways, they become influential and literally shape the future of communications. And they tend to differentiate national responses because the lessons learned are often different cross-nationally.

4. the nation's communications culture, which refers to elite and public beliefs, attitudes, values and habits concerning communications.

The Strength and Interplay of Organized Interests

In all nations, the response to technological change will be determined in part by the relative strength of parties and groups in support of or opposed to particular kinds of new media developments (Dutton & Blumler, 1988). In the United States, the growth of the cable industry was accompanied by its development of a powerful lobbying force in Washington, D. C., which was increasingly capable of competing with more traditional groups representing broadcasters as well as local governments in rewriting national cable policy. Nevertheless, the strength of traditional actors in the communications field (e.g., the broadcasters and PTTs, the post, telegraph, and telecommunications authorities) are central to national responses to technological change in communications. In some respects, technological change has generated conflicts in all major countries by moving previously separate communications industries of print, telephone, broadcasting, and cable out of their traditional niches and into competition. But the new media have brought new actors into the politics of communications policy, including major users of telecommunications, industrial policy elites, and new groups of entrepreneurs.

Cross-nationally, the character and influence of the new communications elite varies. In the United States, the new elites are a different breed, people who are not just interested in broadcasting or publishing. The more established media elite tend to regard themselves first and foremost as communication professionals and advocates of traditional media values. The new elites view themselves as entrepreneurs who have money and who wish to earn more through broadcasting and telecommunications. Although all countries, not only the United States, have an increasing influence of business entrepreneurs as business opportunities emerge around the new media, their influence might be greater in the United States, for example, than in Britain, where the influence of new elites is more circumscribed.

Also, old and new actors in the communications regime may compete differently in particular national settings. In the United States, the Justice Department and the District Court have attempted to create the conditions under which new actors can enter the communications field and compete on a fair basis with industry giants even if appearing at times to place the vitality of the older actors in jeopardy. In Britain, openings have deliberately been created for new actors (such as Mercury and cable system operators) as well as insuring that older actors get a piece of the action.

Another cross-national difference may be the partisan character of debate over communications policy. In the United States, conflicts in the communications area are seldom between political parties. Rather, they are most often between business adversaries (e.g., IBM versus AT&T, and cable versus telephone companies). Because of this, conflicts do not cut as deeply into the social fabric of the society as they do in Germany, nor do they evoke the partisan responses that they do in France and, to a lesser extent, in Britain.

A related dimension of variation concerns societal modes of interest aggregation or methods of conflict resolution. Americans often attempt to resolve conflict through an adversary process in which litigation is the traditional forum where disputes are resolved. The British more often attempt to resolve conflict by finding a comfortable niche for everyone. Often this involves activating the "old boy network" on an informal level. It also requires an ability to bargain, compromise, and adjust as each party seeks to insure its own survival while being mindful of the legitimacy of the other contestants (Blumler, 1987). Japanese modes of interest aggregation are most pronounced in the concern attached to finding mechanisms for achieving a consensus. In part, this concern is rooted in cultural traditions, which place much value in social harmony, perhaps because this is a more realistic goal in Japan as a relatively homogeneous society than in more heterogeneous cultures such as the United States. But consensus is often a pragmatic necessity as well, given the ability of intense minorities to block policy change. Policy elites in Japan are especially sensitive to the views of active and interested parties and make a concerted effort to take a position that maintains the support of all involved.

Institutional Arrangements

Institutional arrangements governing communications have been a traditional criteria of importance to comparative research. The sharpness of old distinctions such as public and private communications sectors are breaking down in the face of changes underway in most nations. But cross-national differences over the role of the state in communications have not been erased. They are still valid to some extent but in more subtly differentiated forms and in complex relations to the marketplace. Cross-national variations mainly concern national administrative and regulatory arrangements, but also the role of local authorities.

A major aspect of control concerns the degree to which national policy making is fragmented or centrally coordinated within the respective nations. The United States is usually singled out for the degree to which a multitude of agencies have partitioned authority over the telecommunications area. Yet all nations exhibit some tensions and conflicts over administrative and planning responsibility in relation to the new technology. Every country has developed relatively independent institutional arrangements for governing the mails, broadcasting, telephone, and cable communications. Advances in information technology have blurred these technological and institutional distinctions such that activities within one policy domain profoundly affect the others. Add to this the growing importance of information technology to economic development and international trade, and an entirely new set of industrial policy elites enter the communications policy arena. Likewise, as communications becomes more central to all public activities, from military to agricultural, programmatic concerns inject other policy elites into the communications area. And while this growing array of actors is not unique to the United States, it manifests itself in more or less unique ways cross-nationally.

Institutional arrangements surrounding communications in the United States reflect an extreme partitioning of authority among federal agencies and branches of government. One manifestation of the more general partitioning of authority in the United States is the Federal Communications Commission (FCC). Other nations have emulated certain aspects of this agency, such as when France created the *Commission Nationale de la Communication et des Libertés* (CNCL). Nevertheless, the FCC remains a unique institution among the advanced, industrial nations (Homet, 1979). Although the FCC is more responsive to groups and interests than its legal-institutional position suggests (Krasnow, Longley, & Terry, 1982), it symbolically and to some extent practically, limits the direct involvement of the national executive and legislative branches in the regulation of communications.

Japan has unique, institutionally anchored conflicts surrounding communications. The political and administrative division in Japan, between the Ministry of International Trade and Industry (MITI) and its agencies, on the one hand, and the Ministry of Posts and Telecommunications (MPT) and its agencies on the other, has affected deliberations over most communications developments underway in Japan (Komatsuzaki, 1987). MPT has traditionally governed telecommunications in Japan, promoting telecommunications as a public service on a universal basis, although the public service monopoly, Nippon Telegraph and Telephone (NTT) has been relatively independent of direct control of the MPT. MITI, which has been broadly concerned with the promotion of Japanese industry and trade since World War II, has been a major driving force behind the development of cable and telecommunications as instruments of international trade and industry (Johnson, 1982). The movement of MITI into the telecommunications arena has led to clashes between these two powerful agencies and their allies (Komatsuzaki, 1987).

In France, notwithstanding the strong position of the French PTT, there have been limits to its role in centralizing control over the new technologies. With respect to the 1982 cable plan, for example, the *Direction General des Telecommunications* (DGT), one of the major directorates of the French P&T, was responsible for the telecommunications infrastructure of the new cable systems. (The other major directorate, *Direction Generale des Postes,* is responsible for postal services.) However, cable projects also involved the National Broadcasting Authority, *Telediffusion de France,* which operated as a public broadcasting monopoly and was to be responsible for the head-ends of the various cable systems. In addition, the *Haute Autorite de la Communication Audiovisuelle,* an independent authority, was to be responsible for allocating frequencies and licensing broadcasters, much like the FCC in the United States, has been established to watch over broadcasters and buffer them from direct governmental control. Other ministries, such as the Ministry of Communications and the Ministry of Culture, were to have roles in cable projects as well. And a temporary agency, *Mission TV-Cable* (an interministerial structure designed to generate a library of programs and spur the development of programming for cable and television), was yet another national actor of relevance. In 1986, with the election of a right of center government, the 1982 cable plan was suspended. But it was replaced with a new scheme for cable system development that decentralized control even further (Vedel & Dutton, 1988), lessening the role of the DGT and giving more discretion to local authorities.

In West Germany, telecommunications and broadcasting have separate institutional arrangements and policies, much as in other nations. The *Deutsche Bundespost* (DBP) is responsible for telecommunications (point-to-point communications) while the *Laender,* comparable to state governments in the United States, are responsible for cultural affairs and broadcasting (Wigand, 1987). What appears rather distinctive about the German case is the degree to which the development of new infrastructures and services like cable have been more centrally directed and bureaucratically managed than this bifurcation of authority would suggest. This is manifested most clearly in the significant role played since the mid-1970s by the Commission for the Development of Telecommunications System (KtK) and since 1982 by Chancellor Kohl's efforts to encourage a greater variety of broadcast programming. Several factors have contributed to greater centralization. First, traditional separations between broadcasting and telecommunications have been imposed on new technologies even when the fit is imperfect. Thus the DBP and Laender have been assigned clear responsibilities with respect to the new media, such as cable. Second, the DBP is a key actor in nearly all new developments, even if playing the role of assistant, and, therefore, serves to coordinate activities ranging from videotext to cable. Third, the legal separation of authority over broadcasting, telecommunications, and new media has created an unusual degree of interdependence among actors. In the case of cable, the DBP is responsible for the network from head-end to the subscriber's property line, whereas artisans responsible for installing television antennae have the right to install subscriber premises equipment for the cable system. This fragmentation of responsibility creates an interdependent versus competitive situation among these two actors.

In contrast to West Germany, Britain may be more institutionally fragmented than first appearances suggest (Blumler, 1987; Tunstall, 1983). The British have developed a more unified and centrally directed approach to communications policy than have the Americans. Yet the number of actors that must be consulted and coordinated to move this central effort forward means that national communications policy has some of the features more commonly associated with the United States. For example, an information technology push has been led by the Ministry of Trade and Industry (DTI), but responsibility for broadcasting falls within the jurisdiction of the Home Office. Moreover, within DTI there is a division of responsibility between telecommunications and information technology, which are handled by different sections. And within the Home Office, responsibilities are divided between the BBC Governors, the Independent Broadcasting Authority and the Cable Authority.

Another major dimension of cross-national variation is in the degree to which local authorities are involved in the new communications technology arrangements. In some countries, they may come close to being a mere object of external manipulation and exploitation for the benefit of policies of other agencies, which may either be public, as in the case of Japan, or private or a mixture, as in the case of Britain, where local authorities have little or no say in the choice of, regulation of, or profit from new cable systems. In some countries they can have a more central role, at least in some sectors, as in the regulation of cable television in the United States. In some places, they are being encouraged to be sources of initiative and decision over how to develop and use cable systems, as is the case in France (Vedel and Dutton, 1988).

Environmental Resources and Constraints

The most obvious but most often ignored cross-national differences among information societies exist in the human, physical, and technological environments that make new cable and telecommunications more valuable and feasible to some nations than to others. But environmental differences also impose constraints on the development of communications technology. Major differences include:

1. the size and wealth of the domestic market,
2. the nature of existing telecommunications infrastructures,
3. the throw-weight of major actors, and
4. a nation's orientation to its international environment.

1. Comparative inquiry highlights differences in the *size and wealth of nations*. The population, geographical space, and wealth of the United States has been of historical importance to the development of its communications industries. Given the size and wealth of its population, and its receptiveness to information and entertainment services, the United States has become the world's largest market for telecommunications products and services. Therefore, it is also a major target of telecommunications industries in the United States (to the point that they have often ignored foreign markets) and abroad. The absolute size of the domestic telecommunications marketplace in Japan is huge as well. Although the nation covers an area only about one and one-half times the size of Oregon, it supports a population nearly half the size of the United States. The domestic market is almost entirely served by Japanese industry.

A related cross-national difference is the vitality of the underlying economy. The British response to information technology might be viewed in light of the gradual but continual decline of its economy since World War II. To many in Britain, the new technology represents little less than an opportunity to pass by competitors that could effectively close Britain out of competition in computing and telecommunications. But in other cases communications seems to be a beneficiary of economic vitality. The periods of greatest economic growth in the United States and Japan have fuelled developments of cable and telecommunications.

2. Another dimension of cross-national comparison is the nature of the *existing telecommunications infrastructure*. The United States has one of the largest investments in existing telecommunications infrastructures. Half of American television households are wired for cable TV,

whereas fewer than 5% of Japanese, British, and French households are linked to multi-channel cable systems (Dutton, Rogers & Jun, 1987). This gives American industry an advantage in the manufacturing and installation of conventional cable networks, but gives other nations an advantage in pursuing new cable system developments. Sunk investments give Americans a special stake in finding ways to modernize existing plant incrementally (for example, efforts to use existing wire pairs and coaxial cable systems for improved voice, data and video communications) as opposed to leapfrogging existing technology. The diffusion of newer technology is more in the interest of nations like France that cannot compete as effectively in older markets, such as the construction of coaxial cable systems, as in the design and manufacture of more state-of-the-art switched, fibre optic technology.

3. Accompanying scale is the *throw-weight of major actors*. The existence of actors in the United States that are capable of making large investments in new ventures plays a major role in differentiating new developments in the United States from those of other countries. First and foremost has been the Department of Defense (DoD), whose programmatic needs have driven research and development within the computer, semi-conductor, and communications sectors at a level far beyond other nations (Nelson, 1984; Weingarten, 1987). Although the relative significance of DoD funding to new communications technology may be declining, its historical role has been unquestionably substantial in the U.S. setting (Mackintosh, 1986). In the private sector, U.S. entrepreneurs are prepared to spend a lot and are willing to lose large sums. This entrepreneurial capability is critical in an area ripe with uncertainty and quite congenial to the American way of ceaseless trial and error in the marketplace as a method of coping with it. Large corporate actors in the United States can risk more on a telecommunications business venture than can some nations of Western Europe.

4. *International orientation* forms a final dimension of comparison relevant to the communications environment. All nations are increasingly affected by developments outside of their own borders. But some countries are more buffeted by international developments than are others. At one extreme, the United States often acts as if it were impervious to developments abroad, unilaterally opening its markets and later raising concerns over telecommunications trade deficits. In contrast, Japan and West Germany appear to gear many long-range policy decisions to the international arena. In Japan, for example, the psychology of resource limitations and logic of natural resource scarcity has contributed to discussions of Japan as a less resource-consuming information society (RITE, 1982). For different reasons, the Federal Republic

of Germany, particularly West Berlin, is also highly sensitive to its international situation. The presence of Allied Forces and their own communications, the island character of Berlin, the beaming of broadcast signals to and from the German Democratic Republic, and the threat of an invasion of American commercial programming combine to make Germany's international situation a unique environmental constraint.

Communication Cultures

Another set of mediating factors stem from national as well as local communications cultures. There are cross-national differences in the time people allocate to media, travel, and leisure activities. For example, variation in the number of hours spent watching television affects the market potential for such services as pay television. In addition, different cultures may vary in their receptivity to advanced technology, engineering feats, the fashioning of ingenious gadgetry—either as sources of value in their own right or as means to other values. Variations in communications cultures include differences in:

1. public receptivity to the media
2. the pluralism of the culture
3. the status accorded consumers of communication services
4. the meaning of communications

1. Nations vary in their *receptivity* to the new media. All advanced, consumer-oriented societies exhibit a certain affinity to high technology when compared to more traditional societies. However, American beliefs and attitudes about communications might reflect a particular receptivity to communications, especially the electronic media and gadgetry that accompanies it. Communications literally makes life swing for many Americans, becoming almost a coin of exchange. Likewise, the Japanese are fond of newspapers, television, video and electronic gadgetry of all sorts. For the French, there are two sides to their communications culture. On the one hand, it appears that the French have far less interest in the media than do Americans or Japanese, for example. The average French household spends less than half the time that an American household spends in front of the TV. On the other hand, the French public has responded positively to Minitel, the French videotex offering. The French may have a more positive orientation to the new media than traditional media habits suggest.

2. The communications cultures of each nation might be compared on the basis of their relative *pluralism*. The American communications

marketplace is not only large. It is also decidedly pluralistic in comparison, for example, with the Japanese marketplace, which is made up of a less diverse array of social, ethnic and racial groups. Industry responses to the American communications market have been towards the provision of more diversified offerings rather than the universal provision of a general service. The development of competition in the provision of new communication technologies has facilitated diversification by permitting the same telephone and cable facilities to support many different kinds of household budgets, needs and preferences. This diversified market orientation is reflected in the range of equipment available for home entertainment and information services: the growth of specialized programming and tiered offerings of cable services. Households vary from those with only basic telephone service to those with a full range of cable and telecommunications equipment and services and everything in between.

3. Cross-nationally, elites vary in the *status accorded the consumer of communications*. Every advanced, consumer-oriented society has become more sensitive to the communications marketplace. Whether paid for directly by consumers, or indirectly through advertising or public subsidy, new telecommunication ventures must be more or less cost justified to the public. It is when the modernization of communication infrastructures is perceived to be the most efficient and economical that support of these projects has been given. However, public responses hold more or less sway in every nation, given different elite perspectives on the status of consumers. One view, most exemplified in the United States, is that of consumer sovereignty. Underlying American traditions is a populist ethic that ordinary people should be the test of all things. In politics, popular sovereignty translates into the legitimacy of the majority at the voting booth. But in telecommunications, it might be called consumer sovereignty. In America, no abstract criteria of technical elegance outweighs the text of the marketplace—public acceptance. Other political-administrative traditions in the United States buttress notions of consumer sovereignty, including first amendment traditions of free speech and press. First amendment traditions have been important historically in minimizing American government involvement in the regulation of the content of communications media and focusing governmental regulation on structural aspects of the media industry (Pool, 1983).

Another view, relatively more skeptical of consumer preferences, is more closely approached by the British. Although there have long been advocates in support of more consumer sovereignty within Britain, as illustrated by recommendations of a committee examining the financing of the BBC (Peacock, 1986), broadcasters in Britain have been less inclined to yield their sovereignty to the consumer. Professional broad-casters in Britain hold that purely commercial, market-oriented concerns should be balanced with if not subordinated to the responsibility to provide programming based on standards of artistic and journalistic excellence (Garnham, 1983; Kuhn, 1986; McCable & Stewart, 1986).

4. The *meaning of communications* also varies cross-nationally. In the United States, communications is a commodity (Schiller, 1981). In Japan, it is that, but also an opportunity for a more participatory, open, and resource independent society (RITE, 1982). In France it has become another symbol and defender of French culture. And in Britain, it has become identified with quality in standards and offerings. In Germany, communications is viewed as a potent and dangerous instrument of power. For such reasons, communications policy remains an extremely sensitive political issue, even relative to other issues in Germany, which has a tradition of fierce political competition.

The meanings attached to communications are rooted in public beliefs and values. Communications is becoming an important commodity in the American marketplace largely because Americans regard communications as no different from other commodities like a loaf of bread or tube of toothpaste. Consumers as well as the policy community have moved from viewing communications as a public good to viewing it as a private commodity (Schiller, 1981). In contrast, Europeans are less inclined to view communications as just another commodity. The British are less likely to play with communications in the same way that Americans and Japanese might do. Like the French, the British take their language very seriously and view public communications, particularly broadcasting, as a very weighty matter. Broadcast innovations quickly become a matter of deliberation, as a potential threat to broadcast standards and values. Thus, compared to Americans or Japanese, the British, Germans, and French are less frivolous in their use of television and the electronic media. Public broadcasting traditions help account for this difference, but it might reflect a more basic difference in the meanings which different national cultures attach to communications.

NATIONAL POLICY

Public policies are not static structures governing the formation and implementation of communications. In many countries, they have changed in response to new technological developments. Examples include the French departure from centralist control, the slackened control over public service regulation of cable television in Britain, the adoption of a new system for governing cable television in Germany, and pressures for deregulation of cable, broadcasting, and common carrier areas within the United States and Japan. As a consequence of such pressures, the traditional dichotomy between market-oriented and state-oriented (or public service agency) societies no longer applies so strictly as it might have seemed in the past. The new technologies are generating pressures for the break-up of established monopolies, diversifications, liberalization, competition, and commercialism in communication orders previously protected from the pressures of the marketplace. This is clearly happening in the cable television sector in Britain, and even in France, elements of liberalism, pragmatism, and commercialism have been injected into formerly highly statist and centralized national cultural policy. How can they be compared?

Broadly, nations vary in how communications infrastructures and services are developed, organized, controlled, and provided. These patterns of development and implementation of communications might be referred to as a nation's communication policy, if policy is defined behaviorally. Policy is often defined narrowly as equivalent to the laws, regulations, and other authoritative rules governing telecommunications and the media (Krasnow, Longley, & Terry, 1982). From this perspective, for example, U.S. cable policy in the late 1980s might be equivalent to the Cable Communications Policy Act of 1984 interpreted in light of relevant judicial rulings and opinions. But policy has a normative and behavioral component as well.[5] Normatively, nations vary in the goals they seek to achieve through communications policy. Behaviorally, they differ in the ways in which communications infrastructures and services are actually developed and implemented (Dutton, Blumler, & Kraemer, 1987; Pressman & Wildavsky, 1973; Salvaggio, 1984). These three aspects of policy (legal, normative, and behavioral) are related but different. For example, a number of European nations have normative policies supportive of the development of information technology, but from a behavioral perspective, they may have institutions and practices in place that discourage such development (Mackintosh, 1986).

Defined in this way, communication policies differ across nations in numerous ways. But there are at least three general categories of com-

[5]Normatively, policy defines ideals and goals which are the target of public policy, such as competition or economic development. Legally, policy is manifested in specific laws, regulations, programs, and other authoritative rules established by relevant governmental authorities, such as the U.S. Cable Communications Policy Act of 1984. Behaviorally, policy is reflected in actual patterns of action, that is, how a cable system is implemented. Throughout, our references to communications policy assume that it is relevant to study public policy at each of these levels.

parison of importance to shaping the social role of communications technology. These are:

1. the scale and quality of developments;
2. the locus of control over the conduits and content of communications, considered separately;
3. the priority given competing values in the development and implementation of communication systems.

Scale and Quality of Development

The status of national developments is a continuing topic of debate and subject to monthly fluctuations. Nevertheless, at any one time it is possible to assess the differing scale and quality of new media infrastructures and services. It is the most visible cross-national manifestation of communication policy approaches. With respect to the scale of multichannel cable television systems, the United States and Japan were early developers of interactive cable projects and made major public and private commitments to them (Dutton, et al., 1987). Since the 1970s, the United States and Canada have wired half or more of their nation's television households, whereas Japan, Britain, France, and West Germany have yet to wire 5% of television households.

Qualitatively, however, national variations are more difficult to measure. Most of the advanced industrial nations have experimented with the development of cable systems built around newer microelectronic and fiber optic technologies, so called "advanced wired city projects," even though no nation has made a major commitment to the wide scale diffusion of such systems (Dutton, et al., 1987). Clearly, the United States and Canadian lead in the scale of cable system development is less pronounced with respect to the quality of new cable system designs and developments. The French with experiments like that in Biarritz (Gerin & Tavernost, 1987) and the Japanese with Hi-Ovis and Mitaka (Kawahata, 1987) rival any other nation in technical sophistication and quality (Dutton, et al., 1987). In the case of more commercial cable system developments, new systems in Britain have yet to reach a large proportion of households, but they are based on technical standards that surpass most American systems.

Locus of Control

Issues of control normally center around the degree to which control over communications is centralized or decentralized. Moreover, it is important to distinguish between two different dimensions of control, namely the content versus the infrastructures of communications. In fact, these two dimensions of control can be used to characterize four ideal types of media structures, as shown in Figure 5.2. A "media monopoly" refers to systems based on the centralized control of both the content and conduits of communications. An "electronic highway" refers to centralized control over the conduits of communications as a common carrier to permit decentralized control over the provision of content. A "network polyarchy" is a system in which control over the conduits is relatively decentralized, while control over content remains centralized. Finally, a system in which both content and conduits are controlled in a decentralized fashion might be called a "network marketplace."

National policies reflect strategic choices to either push towards greater integration of communication infrastructures or to permit, even favor, the growth of more fragmented infrastructures. The United States

CONTROL OVER INFRASTRUCTURE [b]

	CENTRALIZED	DECENTRALIZED
CONTROL OVER CONTENT [c] — CENTRALIZED	Media Monopoly	Network Polyarchy
CONTROL OVER CONTENT [c] — DECENTRALIZED	Electronic Highway	Network Marketplace

a. Adapted from Dutton and others, eds. Wired Cities. Table 1.2.

b. Control and ownership of the physical plant, the communications network, and transmission media.

c. Control and ownership of the content of information and communication services provided over the network(s).

FIGURE 5.2 Alternative Perspectives on Control Over Communications Infrastructure and Content.[a.]

with the private development of cable systems and, especially with the divestiture of AT&T, represents one extreme among nations in the degree to which communication infrastructures are fragmented (Noll, 1984). And nations make choices between more or less integrated infrastructures, as when British cable policy moved towards competitive cable franchises versus the development of a national cable system by British Telecom, for example (Hollins, 1985). But cross-national distinctions are complicated by the fact that some nations, such as Japan, and Britain to a lesser extent, have pursued a more or less mixed strategy. They have encouraged competition in some areas, such as the provision of enhanced telecommunication services, at the same time that they have discouraged it in areas that might lessen discipline over the national telecommunications network.

Control over communications also varies in the degree to which public authorities (versus private industry) assume control in the provision and regulation of services. For example, the degree of public sector involvement in long-range, comprehensive planning efforts varies widely. Although observers in all nations complain about a lack of long-range planning, it is clearly a more visible and important activity in Japan, West Germany and France than it is in the United States, where planning efforts are more confined to the private sector. One difficulty in comparing nations is that planning efforts vary by policy area within particular countries. Long-range comprehensive planning is a hallmark of telecommunications in West Germany, but in the case of broadcasting, German legal traditions and partisan divisions make planning efforts more difficult (Dutton, et al., 1987).

Most generally, the role of government (or public agencies) vis-a-vis the private sector varies across at least three functions: the authoritative, an intermediate role, and umpire. In the first mode, the public organization acts as authoritative decision taker and active provider. Despite the several liberalizing strands, France (the French PTT) and Japan (NTT and MITI) still fit this cell. In the more intermediate role, the public body may act in one or more such roles as enabler, catalyst, orchestrator of other interests and patron. Britain, particularly in the actions of the Department of Trade and Industry in trying to establish the conditions for development of the cable industry, fits in this cell. And in the third case, the state limits its role to regulator or umpire, as in the United States. If governmental goals are realized in this system, it is either because the rules of the game put such goals in the self-interest of the players or because they are served by the goodwill of the providers.

Control over the content and conduits of communications assumes a unique pattern in each nation. Nevertheless, nations vary in the degree to which control is centralized versus decentralized and controlled by public versus private institutions. In the United States, control of both content and conduits is being decentralized most extensively and it has long been among the most privatized. Normatively, policy elites in the United States advocate what might be called a "network marketplace" perspective, in that fragmentation of control over communication infrastructures is accepted as a means for decentralizing control over content (Figure 5.2). Other nations have maintained a closer affinity to communications as an "electronic highway," a view that was prominent in the United States in the 1960s, which assumes a more centralized control over communication infrastructures in order to insure that they operate as a common carrier (Goldmark, 1972; Smith, 1970; Smith, 1972). The French cable plan of 1982, for example, sought to use a national broadband network as a means to decentralize control over the content of communications (Cayrol, 1987; Vedel, 1987). Within Britain, an issue dividing the Labour and Conservative parties in the mid-1980s debate over cable policy was whether a single national cable network should be constructed and controlled by British Telecom or by a number of competing private cable companies. That is, over whether control over the infrastructure of the proposed cable system should be centralized (versus decentralized) and public (versus private).

Priority of Competing Values

Values surface in the purposes for which new communication technologies are promoted. At least four modes surface from observations of information societies (Dutton, et al., 1987). First, an information society may be valued and promoted virtually as a social vision—a desirable way of life in its own right—as it often is promoted in Japan. Second, information technologies may be embraced as focal points for strengthening the country's industrial and commercial stake in international competition, as they are in France, Britain, and Japan. Third, communication technologies may be seen as instruments capable of serving and promoting specific community needs or goals, as in some communities of the United States and Britain (West & Firnberg, 1987). Finally, information technologies may be promoted simply to make a greater profit. The extreme privatization and commercialization of telecommunications in the United States suggests this value and critics of Britain's 1984 cable policy suggested that this was the dominant value in Britain as well (Forester, 1985).

Nations place somewhat different priorities on competing values underlying developments in cable and telecommunications. In some nations, the 'rules of the game' seem to be valued in themselves beyond any specific outcome. In the United States, for example, the push toward deregulation of cable and telecommunications places certain rules of the game, particularly anti-trust, ahead of specific outcomes (Dutton, Dordick, & Phillips, 1984). Nevertheless, outcomes have been important to policy formation in the United States, as when cable system development was supported in part as a means to reinforce the FCC's goal of promoting greater diversity and localism in broadcasting (Negrine, 1985). But, in contrast, British debate over cable policy placed much greater emphasis on certain outcomes, such as programming standards and international trade, than over the rules of the game. Generally, in Britain, France, and Germany, professional broadcasting values have been given more priority than in either the United States or Japan. France, West Germany and, to a lesser extent, Britain have placed a relatively high priority on the media reinforcing their respective cultural traditions and have therefore pursued mechanisms for preventing the importation of foreign programming on the back of new technology. In all nations, international trade and economic development goals have gained priority, but they have been especially salient and influential aspects of the communications policy agenda in Japan and France.

In the United States, the dominance of IBM in the world computer market, the dominance of Hollywood in the film industry, and the security of AT&T in the long distance telephone market may have allowed communications and information technology to be treated as just another commodity. Not until the 1980s has the United States begun to fear the loss of its position in the world communications market as its market shares in world trade declined (Mackintosh, 1986). Mounting trade deficits triggered concern, which has been displayed in discussion over Japan's policies on the importation of telecommunications products. But despite these fears, national defense and other programmatic interests, rather than industrial policy per se have remained the major impetus behind the development of communications technology (Weingarten, 1987).

In Japan, the development of domestic and international commerce in the information and communications arena began early and in earnest. Other nations are more recent converts to the importance of the communications industry to trade and economic development. Prior to this growing economic salience of communications, telecommunications and broadcasting were dominated by elites and values which permitted them to be more isolated from the broader political system.

Also, broad social objectives are often more closely tied and integrated with national policies for communications in Japan and Western Europe than is the case in the United States (Weingarten, 1987). Some countries are taking steps to preserve cultural and social values that might be jeopardized with the development of new communications technologies and services. In France, there is a double concern to limit

foreign material on cable and to subsidize and promote French production sources. But France has by no means been the only nation with
restrictions on foreign media. In the United States, restrictions are
placed on the foreign ownership of broadcast media and in Britain, as
another example, more of a gentleman's agreement between the BBC
and IBA imposes limitations on foreign programming. In Britain,
broadcast authorities have taken measures to preserve public service
broadcasting values in the face of commercial pressures. In Japan, there
continues to be particular concern with cable's public service role, such
as in stimulating greater "community consciousness" (Dutton, et al.,
1987).

SUMMARY AND DISCUSSION

Technological and policy change in communications should generate
interest in comparative inquiry as one approach to understanding the
factors shaping the social role of new communication technology. We
have suggested a framework for examining the many factors within national settings that mediate and differentiate national responses to
technological change in communications. In turn, these responses
shape the social role of communications technology.

We think that the technological revolution in communications requires students of comparative communications to move away from
more conventional frameworks focused on the mass media. Likewise,
students of the new media would benefit from a more explicit comparative perspective rather than treating the communications revolution as a universal phenomena and neglecting the influence of national
settings on the development and impact of the new media.

We've suggested the preliminary outlines of a framework for guiding
comparative analysis of the social shaping of communications
technology. Our framework calls attention to aspects of the national
setting and communications policy that are likely to affect technological
change and its social implications. A focus on new communications
policy rather than on the impacts of the new technologies *per se*, which
have only begun to be implemented on a broad scale, may be more
useful at this point in time. The adolescence of the new media makes
assessments of their impacts highly speculative.

Nevertheless, there are major difficulties confronting the comparative
study of technological change. One is conceptual. A major goal of comparative research is to replace the names of nations or other social
systems with the names of variables (Przeworski & Teune, 1970). Of
course, much of the practice of comparative research remains far from
that goal. In communications particularly, we continue to use the names

of nations as labels for complex patterns of variation for which variable names cannot be easily substituted. The present discussion only makes a few preliminary moves in the direction of specifying categories and dimensions of variation. Much conceptual work remains to be done.

Another problem is a more empirical one of adequately measuring national variations. There are a number of more or less reliable indicators of the development and use of communications (e.g., the number of households subscribing to cable). But many aspects of communications policy and the national setting are not readily measured and must be studied from a more qualitative/historical perspective.

In summary, a comparative framework should guide more discussions of the information society because it focuses attention on how and why nations respond differently to the problems and opportunities posed by new technology. What factors mediate and differentiate responses to these rather universal technological developments? What consequences will these national contexts have on the way in which communications infrastructures and services are provided? And what consequences for society result from national responses to technological change? Although there are practical, conceptual, and methodological difficulties in pursuing comparative research, this perspective provokes a set of questions that should be addressed in discussions of the information society.

REFERENCES

Blumler, J. G. (1987). Live and let live: The politics of cable. In W. H. Dutton, J. G. Blumler, & K. L. Kraemer (Eds.), *Wired cities: Shaping the future of communications*. Boston, MA: G. K. Hall.

Cayrol, R. (1987). The post-1981 national policy context for new communication technologies. In W. H. Dutton, J. G. Blumler, & K. L. Kraemer (Eds.), *Wired cities: Shaping the future of communications*. Boston, MA: G. K. Hall.

Danziger, J. N., Dutton, W. H., Kling, R., & Kraemer, K. L. (1982). *Computers and politics: High technology in American local governments*. New York: Columbia University Press.

Dordick, H. S., Bradley, H. G., & Nanus, B. (1980). *The emerging network marketplace*. Norwood, NJ: Ablex Publishing Corporation.

Dutton, W. H. (1987). The politics of cable policy in Britain. Paper presented at the Annual Meeting of the American Political Science Association, Chicago, Illinois, September 3–6, 1987.

Dutton, W. H., & Blumler, J. G. (1988). The faltering development of cable television in Britain, *International Political Science Review, 9*, 4, 279–303.

Dutton, W. H., Blumler, J. G., & Kraemer, K. L. (Eds.). (1987). *Wired cities: Shaping the future of communications*. Boston, MA: G. K. Hall.

Dutton, W. H., Dordick, H., & Phillips, A. (1984). Perspectives on national cable policy: Focusing the issues. *Telematics and Informatics, 1*(2) (March–April), 153–170.

Dutton, W. H., & Kraemer, K. L. (1985). *Modeling as negotiating*. Norwood, NJ: Ablex.

Dutton, W. H., Rogers, E. M., Jun, S. (1987). The diffusion and impacts of information technology in households, *Oxford Surveys in Information Technology*, vol. 4, 133–193.

Edelstein, A. S., Bowes, J. E., & Harsel, S. M. (1978). *Information societies: Comparing the Japanese and American experiences*. Seattle, WA: International Communication Center, University of Washington.

Ferguson, M. (Ed.). (1986). *New communication technologies and the public interest: Comparative perspectives on policy and research*. London: Sage Publications.

Forester, T. (1985). The cable that snapped. *New Society*, 24, 133–135.

Garnham, N. (1983). Public service versus the market, *Screen*, (24), 1, 6–27.

Gerin, F., & Tavernost, N. de. (1987). Biarritz and the future of videocommunications. In W. H. Dutton, J. G. Blumler, & K. L. Kraemer (Eds.), *Wired cities: Shaping the future of communications*. Boston, MA: G. K. Hall.

Goldmark, P. C. (1972). Communication and the community. A Scientific American Book, *Communication*. San Francisco, CA: W. H. Freeman.

Greenberger, M. (Ed.). (1985). *Electronic publishing plus*. White Plains, NY: Knowledge Industries Publications.

Hollins, T. (1985). *Beyond broadcasting: Into the cable age*. London: Broadcasting Research Unit, British Film Institute.

Homet, R. S. (1979). *Politics, cultures, and communication*. New York: Praeger.

Johnson, C. (1982). *MITI and the Japanese miracle*. Stanford, CA: Stanford University Press.

Kawahata, M. (1987). Hi-Ovis. In W. H. Dutton, J. G. Blumler, & K. L. Kraemer (Eds.), *Wired cities: Shaping the future of communications*. Boston, MA: G. K. Hall.

Komatsuzaki, S. (1987). The Japanese scene. In W. H. Dutton, J. G. Blumler, & K. L. Kraemer (Eds.), *Wired cities: Shaping the future of communications*. Boston, MA: G. K. Hall.

Kuhn, R. (1986). Deregulation in broadcasting: The case of Great Britain. Paper presented at the International Conference on Deregulation in Telecommunications & Broadcasting, Paris, May 27–29.

Krasnow, E. G., Longley, L. D., & Terry, H. A. (1982). *The politics of broadcast regulation*. Third Edition. New York: St. Martin's Press.

McQuail, D., & Siune, K. (Eds.) (1986). *New media politics: Comparative perspectives in western Europe*. London: Sage Publications.

MacCable, C., & Stewart, O. (Eds.) (1986). *The BBC and public service broadcasting*. Manchester, Britain: University of Manchester Press.

Mackintosh, I. (1986). *Sunrise Europe: The dynamics of information technology*. New York: Basil Blackwell.

Martin, J. (1974). *The wired society*. Englewood Cliffs, NJ: Prentice-Hall, Inc.

Nelson, R. R. (1984). *High technology politics: Five-nation comparison*. Washington, DC: American Enterprise Institute for Public Policy Research.

Negrine, R. M. (Ed.) (1985). *Cable television and the future of broadcasting*. London: Croom Helm.

Noll, M. (1984). A personal perspective on the fragmentation of the Bell system. Los Angeles, CA: Annenberg School of Communications. Unpublished manuscript.

Peacock, A. (1986). *Report of the committee on financing the BBC*. London: Her Majesty's Stationery Office.

Pool, I. de Sola. (1983). *Technologies of freedom*. Cambridge, MA: Harvard University Press.

Porat, M. U. (1978). Communication policy in an information society. In A. C. Robinson (Ed.), *Communications for tomorrow*. New York: Praeger.

Pressman, J. L., & Wildavsky, A. B. (1973). *Implementation*. Berkeley, CA: University of California Press.

Przeworski, A., & Teune, H. (1970). *The logic of comparative social inquiry*. New York: Wiley-Interscience.

RITE. (1982). *A vision of telecommunications policy in the '80s*. Tokyo, Japan: Research Institute of Telecommunications and Economics.

Rogers, E. M. (1986). *Communication technology.* New York: The Free Press.
Rogers, E. M., & Balle, F. (Eds.) (1985). *The media revolution in America and western Europe.* Norwood, NJ: Ablex Publishing Corporation.
Rogers, E. M., & Larson, J. (1984). *Silicon valley fever.* New York: The Free Press.
Salvaggio, J. (1981). **copy coming

Schiller, H. (1981). *Who knows?* Norwood, NJ: Ablex Publishing Corporation.
Smith, R. L. (1970). The wired nation, *The Nation,* May 18, pp. **-**.
Smith, R. L. (1972). *The wired nation: Cable TV: The electronic communications highway.* New York: Harper and Row.
Tunstall, J. (1983). *The media in Britain.* London: Constable.
Vedel, T. (1987). Local policies for wiring France. In W. H. Dutton, J. G. Blumler, & K. L. Kraemer (Eds.), *Wired cities: Shaping the future of communications.* Boston, MA: G. K. Hall.
Vedel, T., & Dutton, W. H. (1988). New media politics: Shaping cable television in France. Los Angeles, CA: Annenberg School of Communications, unpublished paper.
Weingarten, F. (1987). The R&D push. In W. H. Dutton, J. G. Blumler, & K. L. Kraemer (Eds.), *Wired cities: Shaping the future of communications.* Boston, MA: G. K. Hall.
West, D. & Firnberg, D. (1987). Milton Keynes. In W. H. Dutton, J. G. Blumler, & K. L. Kraemer (Eds.), *Wired cities: Shaping the future of communications.* Boston, MA: G. K. Hall.
Whisler, T. L. (1967). The impact of information technology on organizational control. In C.A. Meyers (Ed.), *The impact of computers on management* (pp. 16–60). Cambridge, MA: MIT Press.
Wigand, R. (1987). The national policy context. In W. H. Dutton, J. G. Blumler, & K. L. Kraemer (Eds.), *Wired cities: Shaping the future of communications.* Boston, MA: G. K. Hall.
Woolgar, S. (1985). Why not a sociology of machines? *Sociology, 19*(4), 557–572.

6 Communication Technology: For Better or for Worse?

DANIEL BELL
Harvard University

Human societies have seen four distinct revolutions in the character of social interchange: speech, writing, printing and, now, telecommunication. Each revolution is associated with a distinctive, technologically-based, way of life.

Speech was central to the hunting-and-gathering bands—the signals that allowed men to act together in common pursuits. Writing was the foundation of the first urban settlements in agricultural society—the basis of record keeping and the codified transmission of knowledge and skills. Printing was the thread of industrial society—the basis of widespread literacy and the foundation of mass education. Telecommunications (from the Greek *tele,* "over a distance")—the ties of cable, radio, telegraph, telephone, television, and newer technologies—is the basis of an *information society.*

Human societies exist because they can purposefully coordinate the activities of their members. (What is a corporation if not a social invention for the coordination of men, material, and markets for the mass production of goods?) Human societies prosper when, through peaceful transactions, goods and services can be exchanged in accordance with the needs of individuals.

Central to all this is information. Information comprises everything from news of events to price signals in a market. The success of an enterprise depends in part on the rapid transmission of accurate information.

The foundation of the Rothschild fortune was advance information by carrier pigeon of the defeat of Napoleon at Waterloo, so that the

89

Rothschilds could make quicker stock market decisions. (The rapidity of transmission of information on companies today is responsible for the random walk theory of stock market prices, because such rapidity minimizes the time advantage of inside information.)

General equilibrium theory in economics is dependent on "perfect information," so that buyers and sellers know the full range of available prices on different goods and services, and the markets are cleared on the basis of relative prices and ordinal utilities. What was once possible by walking around a local market now has to be done through complex transmission of news, which flashes such information to clients in "real time."

All facets of society are concerned with information—from balance-of-trade figures to money supply, birthrates, interregional shifts, changes of buying tastes and habits—should recognize more readily than any other the importance of any changes in the type and character of information. For this reason, we should understand the nature and extent of the powerful technological revolution that will escort us into the information era, as well as its potentialities and threats.

A NEW COMMUNICATION SYSTEM

In the 1980s, more than 130 years after the creation of the first effective telecommunication device, telegraphy, we are on the threshold of a new development that, by consolidating all such devices and linking them to computers, earns the name of a "revolution" because of the various possibilities of communication that are now unfolding. This is what Nora and Minc, in an extraordinary report to the president of the French Republic, call telematique, or what Anthony Oettinger calls communications (Minc & Nora, 1978).

Telematique, or communications, is the merging of telephone, computers, and television into a single yet differentiated system that allows for transmission of data and interaction between persons or between computers through cables, microwave relays, or satellites. Thus, communication becomes faster, but it also is organized in a totally new way. It would be far beyond the scope of this essay to suggest some of the basic communication modes in an information society and illustrate the consequences.

Data processing networks. These would register purchases made in stores automatically through computer terminals as bank transfers. Orders for goods, such as automobiles, would be sent through computer networks and transformed into a programming and scheduling series to provide for individual specifications of the items ordered. In a broad sense, this could be a replacement of much of the "paper economy" by an electronic transfer system.

Information banks and retrieval systems. In an information society these would recall or search for information through computer systems and would print out a legal citation, a chemical abstract, census data, market research material, and the like.

Teletext systems. In these systems, such as the British Post Office Prestel system (formerly called View Data), or the French Tic-tac and Antiope systems, news, weather, financial information, classified advertisements, catalog displays, and research material are displayed on home television consoles, representing a combination of the yellow pages of telephone books, the classified advertisements of newspapers, standard reference material, and news.

Facsimile systems. Here, documents and other material (invoices, orders, mail) can be sent electronically rather than by postal systems.

Interactive on-line computer networks. These allow research teams, office managers, or government agencies to maintain communication so as to translate new research results, orders or, perhaps, financial information into further action (Bell, 1977).

These are not speculations or science fiction fantasies; they are developed technologies and will be central to information societies. The rate of introduction and diffusion will vary on the basis of cost and competition of rival modes and on government policies that will either facilitate or inhibit some of these developments.

The rate of diffusion is further compounded by capital problems: The need for a large-scale shift to new, independent sources of energy requires a large, disproportionate allocation of capital to purposes that are, inherently, capital-using rather than capital-saving. Thus the marginal efficiency of capital (as reflected in social capital-output rations) tends to fall. The uncertainty of inflation leads, sometimes, to the postponement of capital investment or the short-term substitution of labor inputs rather than capital inputs, thus dragging down further a society's total productivity. These are economic and political questions that, again, are outside the scope of this article.

If we assume, however, that many of these new technologies and modes will eventually be introduced, what can we say of their consequences? It is hazardous, if not impossible, to predict specific social changes and outcomes. What one can do is to sketch broad social changes that are likely to occur when these new modes are all in use. And that is the purpose of the following two sections.

SOCIETAL INFRASTRUCTURE

Every society is tied together by three different kinds of infrastructure:
transportation, energy grids, and communication.

Modes of Transportation

The oldest of these infrastructures is transportation, which first took
place by trails, roads, and rivers, and later by canals. Trade was the
means of breaking down the isolation of villages and served as a means
of communication between distant areas. Thus, transport has been the
major linkage between settled areas.

Because of transport requirements, all the major cities of the world
have been built near water. The industrial heartland of the United States,
for example, was created by the interplay of resources and water
transport.

Thus, the iron ore from the Mesabi Range could move on Lake
Superior, and coal in southern Illinois and western Pennsylvania could
be tied to the Great Lakes by a river system. Such a network allowed
the development of a steel and then an automobile industry. The water
transport system served to thread together the industrial cities of
Chicago, Detroit, Cleveland, Buffalo, and Pittsburgh.

In Germany, in the early 18th and 19th centuries, most commerce
flowed from north and south because of the course of the major rivers
such as the Rhine, Elbe, Oder, and Weser. The coming of the railroad,
linking east and west, greatly facilitated the unification of Germany by
1870 and its development as an industrial and military power.

Power Sources

The second infrastructure is energy. At first, waterwheels on rivers were
used for power, followed by hydroelectricity, then oil, gas, and electricity.

The interaction of the energy and transport systems allowed for the
spread of industries and towns because electricity grids could transmit
power over hundreds of miles. The result was the development of large
industrial complexes occupying vast spaces through the long-distance
transmission of energy.

Communications Systems

The oldest communication infrastructure is the postal service. The development of the various telecommunications systems began much later.

In an information society it is likely that there will be a major shift in the relative importance of the infrastructures: telecommunications will be the central infrastructure tying together a society. Such a network increases personal interaction and drastically reduces the costs of distance. It affects the location of cities because the external economies—gains because of proximity, such as in advertising, printing, and legal services for banks—once possible only in central city districts are being replaced by communication devices.

Most important, an information society enlarges the arenas in which social action takes place. It is only since 1950 that many countries, because of revolutions in air transport and communication, have become national societies, in which impacts in any one part of the national society are immediately felt in any other part.

In the broadest sense, we have for the first time a genuine international economy where prices and money values are known in real time in every part of the globe. Thus, for example, treasurers of banks or controllers of corporations can subscribe to a Reuters international money market service and obtain, in real time, quotations on different currencies in 25 different money markets from Frankfurt to London to New York to Tokyo to Singapore to Hong Kong, so that they can take advantage of the different rates and move their holdings about.

By satellite communication, through television, every part of the world is immediately visible to every other part. The multiplication of interactions and the widening of the social arenas are the major consequences of a shift in the modalities of the infrastructure. This problem will be discussed later.

POSTINDUSTRIAL SOCIETY

The creation of an information society also speeds the development of what I have called a postindustrial society (Bell, 1973). Table 6.1 schematically compares preindustrial, industrial, and postindustrial types of developments.

Most of the world—that is, principally the countries in Asia, Africa, and Latin America—is preindustrial in that 60% or more of its labor force is engaged in extractive industries. The life of these countries is a "game against nature," in which national wealth depends on the quality of the natural resources and vicissitudes of world commodity prices.

A smaller section of the world, the countries around the North Atlantic littoral plus the Soviet Union and Japan, is made up of industrial countries where the fabrication of goods, by the application of machine technology with energy, is the basis of wealth and economic growth.

Some of these latter countries are moving into the postindustrial

TABLE 6.1 The Postindustrial Society: A Comparative Scheme

Modes	Preindustrial	Industrial	Postindustrial
Mode of production	Extractive	Fabrication	Processing & recycling services
Economic sector	Primary	Secondary	Tertiary
	Agriculture	Goods producing	Transportation
	Mining	Durables	Utilities
	Fishing	Nondurables	
	Timber	Heavy construction	Quaternary
	Oil & Gas		Trade
			Finance
			Insurance
			Real estate
			Quinary
			Health
			Research
			Recreation
			Education
			Government
Transforming resource	Natural power-wind, water, draft animal-human muscle	Created energy-electricity, oil, gas, coal, nuclear power	Information*-computer & data transmission systems
Strategic resource	Raw materials	Financial capital	Knowledge**
Technology	Craft	Machine technology	Intellectual technology
Skill base	Artisan, farmer, manual worker	Engineer, semiskilled worker	Scientist, technical & professional occupations
Methodology	Common sense, trial & error, experience	Empiricism, experimentation	Abstract theory; models, simulations, decision theory, systems analysis
Time perspective	Orientation to the past	Ad hoc adaptiveness experimentation	Future orientation, forecasting & planning
Design	Game against nature	Game against fabricated nature	Game between persons
Axial principle	Traditionalism	Economic growth	Codification of theoretical knowledge

*Broadly, data processing. The storing, retrieval, and processing of data become the essential resource for all economic and social exchanges.

**An organized set of statements of facts or ideas, presenting a reasoned judgment or experimental result, that is transmitted to others through some communication medium in some systematic form.

world. In the postindustrial state, first there is a shift from the production of goods to the selling of services. Services exist in all societies, but in preindustrial societies they are primarily domestic services. In industrial societies, they are ancillary to the production of goods, such as transportation, utilities, and financial services. In postindustrial societies, the emphasis is on human services (education, health, social services) and professional services (computing, systems analysis, and scientific research and development).

The second dimension of postindustrial society is more important: For the first time, innovation and change derive from the codification of theoretical knowledge. Every society has its base, to some extent, in knowledge, but technical change has now become dependent on the codification of theoretical knowledge. We can see this easily by examining the relation of technology to science.

Steel, automotive, utilities, and aviation industries are primarily of the 19th century in that they were created largely by inventors—"talented tinkerers"—who knew little about the basic laws or findings of science. This was true of such a genius as Edison, who invented the electric lamp, the gramophone or record player, and the motion picture, among other things. Yet he knew little of the work of Maxwell or Faraday on electromagnetism, the union of whose two fields was the basis of almost all subsequent work in modern physics. This was equally true of Siemens with his invention of the dynamo, and Bell with the telephone, or Marconi with the radio wireless.

The first modern industry is chemistry, in that the scientist must have a knowledge of the theoretical properties of the macromolecules that he is manipulating in order to know where he is going. What is true of all science-based industries of the last half of the 20th century, and the products that come from them, is that they derive from work in theoretical science, and it is theory that focuses the direction of future research and the development of products.

The crucial point about a postindustrial society is that knowledge and information become the strategic and transforming resources of the society, just as capital and labor have been the strategic and transforming resources of industrial society. The crucial variable for any society, therefore, is the strength of its basic research and science and technological resources—in its universities, in its research laboratories, and in its capacity for scientific and technological development.

In these respects, the new information technology becomes the basis of a new intellectual technology in which theoretical knowledge and its new techniques (such as systems analysis, linear programming, and probability theory), hitched to the computer, become decisive for industrial and military innovation.

COROLLARY PROBLEMS

Two important consequences of the revolution in telecommunications round out the picture of social change. One is that, because of a combination of market and political forces, a new international division of labor is taking place in the world economy; the other involves a widening scale of political effects across the world.

Economic Changes

The developing countries, in proclaiming a new international economic order at Lima in 1975, have demanded that 25% of the world's manufacturing capacity be in the hands of the Third World by the year 2000. This is a highly unrealistic target. Yet some tidal changes are already taking place.

There is one group of developing countries—among them Brazil, Mexico, South Korea, Taiwan, Singapore, Algeria, Nigeria—that is beginning to industrialize rapidly. It is likely that in the future, traditional routinized manufacturing, such as the textile, shipbuilding, steel, shoe, and small consumer appliances industries, will be drawn out of the advanced industrial countries and become centered in this new tier.

The response of the advanced industrial countries will be either protectionism and the disruption of the world economy or the development of a comparative advantage in, essentially, the electronic and advanced technological and science-based industries that are the feature of a postindustrial society. How this development takes place will be a major issue of economic and social policy for the nations of the world.

Expanded Political Arena

The second, more subtle, yet perhaps more important, problem is that the revolution in telecommunications necessarily means a change in scale—an expansion in the political arenas of the world, the drawing in of new claimants, and the multiplication of actors or constituencies.

We have heard much of the acceleration of the pace of change. It is seductive but ultimately a meaningless idea other than as a metaphor. For one has to ask, "Change of what?" and, "How does one measure the pace?" There is no metric that applies in general, and the word change is ambiguous.

As Mervyn Jones, the English author, once pointed out, a man who was born in 1800 and died in 1860 would have seen the coming of the railway, the steamship, the telegraph, gas lighting, factory-made objects, and the expansion of the large urban centers. A man who was born in 1860 and died in 1920 would have seen the telephone, electric lights, automobile, and motion pictures. He might be familiar with the ideas of Darwin, Marx, and Freud. He would have seen the final destruction of most monarchies, the expansion of the ideas of equality, and the rise and breakup of imperialism.

How does one measure the events of the past 40 years in order to say that the pace of change has increased? If anything, one might say that because growth is never exponential in a linear way but follows an S-shaped or logistic curve, we are close to leveling off many of the so-called changes that have transformed our lives (e.g., transport and communication will not increase appreciably in speed). As world population increases, we seem to have now passed the point of inflection—that midway point where the S-curve of change is now slowing down.

But what is definite is that the scale of change has widened. And a change in scale, as physicists and organization theorists have long known, requires essentially a change in form. The growth of an enterprise, for example, requires specialization and differentiation and very different kinds of control and management systems when the scales move from, say, $10 million to $100 million to $1 billion.

The problem becomes politically acute for political systems. Rousseau, in The Social Contract, set for a "natural law" that the larger a state becomes, the more its government will be concentrated, so that the number of rulers decreases as the population increases. Rousseau was seeking to show that a regime necessarily changes form as the population increases, as the interactions between people multiply, and as interests become more complicated and diverse.

The problem for future information societies—especially those that wish to maintain democratic institutions, the control of government by the consent of the people, and an expanding degree of participation—is to match the scales between political and economic institutions and activities. The fact that government has become more distant from and yet more powerful in the lives of persons has led increasingly, to separatism, localism, and breakaway movements in society.

At the same time, the scale of economic activities on a worldwide canvas has indicated that we lack the governing mechanisms to deal with, for example, monetary problems, commodity prices, and industrial relocation on the new scales on which these actions take place. For many countries, the national state is becoming too big for the small problems of life and too small for the big problems of life (Bell, 1977a; De Jouvenel, 1967).

IMPLICATIONS FOR PERSONAL LIBERTY

All of these structural changes lead to the pointed question of the fate of individual and personal liberties in this "brave new world." We have had, from Aldous Huxley to George Orwell, dire predictions of the kinds of controls—the expansion of Big Brother totalitarianism—that may be coming as a result of such technological changes. Indeed, an old Russian joke asks: Who is Stalin? Answer: Genghis Khan with a telephone. There are many humorous examples of how the new technologies permit the growth of scrutiny mechanisms and intrusions in personal life.

A story in the London *Times* on the growth of security procedures in Germany reports that the movements of a German business consultant, who has to cross the border into Switzerland several times a day, were reported to a computer center so that he suddenly found himself on a list of persons to be watched. But the moral of the story is not that the computerization of the border crossings increases the power of the police, but that because of the political threats of terrorism such procedures had to be adopted.

The issue of social control can be put under three headings:

1. Expansion of the techniques of surveillance.
2. Concentration of the technology of record keeping.
3. Control of access to strategic information by monopoly or government imposition of secrecy.

In all three areas there has been an enormous growth of threatening powers and, in a free society such as ours, a growing apprehension about their misuse.

The techniques of surveillance, because they are the most dramatic, have received the most attention. In George Orwell's *1984*, the government of Oceana monitors party members by a remote sensor of human heartbeats. The sensors are located in the two-way television screens in all homes, government offices, and public squares. By tuning in on individuals and measuring their heartbeats, Big Brother can discover whether an individual is engaged in unusual activities.

A young physiologist has already discovered, to his dismay, that he had invented such a device himself. Seeking to measure the physiological activities of salamanders less painfully than by plugging painful electrodes into the animals' bodies, he created a delicate voltage sensor that measures the extremely minute electrical field that surrounds the bodies of all living organisms so that one can now detect, and record from a distance, an animal's heartbeat, respiration, muscle tension, and body movements. When he was told that he had invented the device that Orwell imagined, he made a study of the predictions Orwell made in *1984* and found that, of the 137 devices Orwell had described, some 100 are now practical (Goodman, 1978). Also, in Solzhenitsyn's *First Circle*, it may be recalled, the prisoner-scientists in the secret police laboratory were working on devices to identify telephone callers by voiceprints and also to unscramble coded telephone conversations—devices that are in use today.

The computerization of records, which intelligence agencies, police, and credit agencies use, is by now quite far advanced, and so much so that individuals are constantly being warned to check to see that their credit ratings are accurately recorded in computer memories, lest they be cut off, especially in cashless and checkless transactions, from the purchase of goods that they need. The problem of secrecy is old and persistent. *Science* magazine has reported that at the request of the National Security Agency (NSA), the Department of Commerce imposed a secrecy order that inhibited commercial development of a communication device, invented by a group in Seattle, for which a patent had been applied. The technique involved in the patent application goes beyond the voice-scrambler technology used in police and military communication and takes advantage of the spread-spectrum communication band to expand the range of citizen's band and maritime radios. *Science* reports:

> The inventors are fighting to have the order overturned so that they can market their device commercially. They regard their struggle as a test of whether the government will allow the burgeoning of cheap, secure communications technology to continue in the private sector or whether it will keep a veil of secrecy over the work—effectively reserving it exclusively for military and intelligence applications. (*Science*, 1978)

Real as these issues are for liberty in the personal and economic sense, they are not the true locus of the problem. It is not in the technology per se but in the social and political system in which that technology is embedded.

The most comprehensive system of surveillance was invented by that malign individual Joseph Fouche, who served as police chief for Napoleon I. A former Catholic priest, Fouche became a militant leader of the French Revolution, having directed the massacre at Lyons, and after Napoleon he continued as police chief during the Bourbon restoration of Louis XVIII. Fouche was the first to organize every *concierge* in Paris as an agent of the police and to report to local headquarters the movements each day of every resident of the buildings.

The scale of operations has expanded since Fouche's day. Technology is an instrument for keeping abreast of the management of scale. The point can be made more abstractly, yet simply. Technology does not determine social structure; it simply widens all kinds of possibilities. Technology is embedded in a social support system, and each social structure has a choice as to how it will be used. Both the Soviet Union and the United States are industrial societies, using much the same kind of technology in their production systems. Yet the organization of industry, and the rights of individuals, vary greatly in the two societies.

One can take the same technology and show how different social support systems use them in very different ways. For the automobile, one can show very different patterns of use, and consequent social costs, without changing a single aspect of the automobile itself. Thus, in one kind of society, one can have a system of complete private ownership of the automobile where the individual can come and go largely at his own pleasure. But such a pattern involves a high cost to the individual for the purchase of the car, the insurance, gasoline and depreciation, as well as a cost to the community for more roads, parking garages, and the like.

One can envisage a very different pattern, which some cities have tried, where automobiles are barred from a large area, and in their place there is a "public utility" system in which an individual subscribes to a car service. He goes a short distance—no farther, say, than a usual bus stop—to a parking lot, takes a car, using a magnetic coded key, drives off in that car to his destination, and simply leaves the car in that other lot, again no farther than a bus stop distance from where he wants to go.

The user has a great degree of mobility (as with a taxi service, yet without the cost of a driver), but fewer cars are needed in this kind of distributive system. The cost to the individual is the walk to and from the parking lot and the brief wait for a car that may be necessary if there are shortages.

Such a system represents an expansion of the car-hire service that is available at airports and throughout cities in many countries. The illustration is trivial, yet the import of the example is not so trivial: A single technology is compatible with a wide variety of social patterns and the decisions about the use of the technology are, primarily, a function of the social pattern a society chooses.

To expand this proposition, the following theorem holds: The revolution in telecommunications makes possible both an intense degree of centralization of power, if the society decides to use it in that way, and large decentralization because of the multiplicity, diversity, and cheapness of the modes of communication.

It is quite clear that an elaborate telecommunications system allows for intensification of what in military parlance is called command and control systems. Through such systems, the U.S. Air Force was able to set up a watch pattern that kept track of all aircraft or unidentified flying objects over the North American air space and relayed that information, in real time, to a centralized control station that in turn monitored the information.

Without such a system, one could not have basic security against an enemy attack. Yet, in the Vietnam war, the development of the command and control system meant that tactical decisions, which in the past were made by field commanders, were often made on the basis of political decisions in Washington. The Vietnam war was an extraordinary instance of the centralization of military decisions on a scale rarely seen before.

In Chile, from 1971 to 1973, the British organization theorist Stafford Beer set up an effort to prepare a single computer program to model (and eventually control) every level of the Chilean economy. Under his direction, with the cooperation of the Allende government, an operations room was created to plan for centralized control of Chilean industry. This was not a simulations model, as used by Jay Forrester and his associates to demonstrate what might be if certain assumptions held, but an operational recursive model (i.e., a set of "nestings" or minisystems built into a pattern of larger systems) to direct the course of the economy from a single center. Whether this would have been possible is moot; the effort was cut short by the overthrow of the Allende government in September 1973.

However, by the very same technology, one could go in wholly different directions. Through the expansion of two-way communication, as in various cable television systems, one could have a complete "plebiscitarian" system whereby referenda on a large variety of issues could be taken through responses back from computer terminals in each house. For some persons this would be complete democracy; for others it might mean a more manipulative society, or even the tyranny of the majority, or an increase in the volatility of political discussion and conflict in society.

Without going to either extreme (and, at times, the extremes meet), it is clear that the revolution in telecommunications allows for a large diversity of cultural expressions and enhancement of different life styles simply because of the increase in the number of channels available to people. This is happening in radio, for example, where stations cater to very different tastes, from rock to classical music, from serious talk shows to news and game shows. With the multiplication of television channels and of videocassette, the variety of choice becomes staggering.

Under free conditions, individuals can create their own modes of communication and their own new communities. No one, for example, foresaw the mushrooming of citizens' band radios and the ways in which they came to be used. These allow strangers to communicate readily with one another. The first, fascinating, social pattern was the development of an informal communication and warning system by truckers on the major roadways, warning one another of traps by law enforcement agents or of road conditions ahead. Sometimes truckers simply used the CB radio to enlarge social ties in what is an essentially lonely occupation.

The CB radio has become a major means of communication in isolated village areas, as in Nova Scotia—a form of community telephone line. And, with a two-way video cable television, community interchange may become possible between the elderly or hobby enthusiasts or others with special interests and needs.

In a larger political sense, the extension of networks because of metaphoric face-to-face contact will mean that political units can be reorganized more readily to match, and be responsive to, the scales of the appropriate social unit, from neighborhood to region.

In the end, the question of the relation of technology to liberty is both prosaic and profound. It is prosaic because the technology is primarily a facilitator or a constraint, available to intensify or to enhance—whichever direction a political system chooses to go. It is profound because man is a creature capable both of compassion and of murder. Which path is chosen goes back to the long, agonized efforts of civilized communities to find institutional arrangements that can allow individuals to realize their potentials and that respect the integrity of the person.

In short, the question of liberty is, as always, a political consideration. Even speaking of threats to liberty because of the powerful nature of the new surveillance technologies is a misstatement; such a view focuses on technological gadgetry rather than on organizational realities.

Orwell, with his powerful imagination, could conjure up a Big Brother watching all others. But there is not, and cannot be, a single, giant brain that absorbs all information. In most instances, the centralization of such controls simply multiplies bureaucracies, each so cumbersome and jealous of its prerogatives (look at the wars between intelligence agencies in the United States) as to inhibit, often, the effective use of information.

If anything, the real threat of such technological megalomania lies in the expansion of regulatory agencies whose rising costs, bureaucratic regulations, and delays inhibit innovation and change in a society. In the United States, at least, it is not Big Brother, but Slothful Brother, that becomes the problem.

I do not mean to minimize the potential for abuse in our information society—it does exist. But there are also agencies of concern, such as the press.

The crucial issues are access to information and the restriction of any monopoly on information, subject, under stringent review, to genuine concerns of national security. The Freedom of Information Act of the 1960s was the fruit of a long campaign to open up the records of government agencies so that individuals would have access to information about themselves or information about government agency activities involving public matters.

In a somewhat different context, when the first large computers were created, technologists compared them to large generators distributing energy and assumed that the most efficient model of computer use would be regulated computer utilities, which would sell computer time or data services to users. The rapidity of technological change, resulting in the multiplication of mini- and microcomputers, as well as some second thoughts about the diverse markets for computer usage, led to complete abandonment of the ideas of computer utilities and recognition of the competitive market as the best framework for computer development.

The possible growth of the teletext systems described earlier, of cable television and videocassettes, may lead to the upheaval of the major television network systems and to new modes of news presentation, similar to the new competition AT&T faces today in transmission systems.

In sum, from all this arises a moral different from what we might expect. Although technology *is* instrumental, the free and competitive use of various technologies in an information society is one of the best means of breaking up monopolies, public and private, and that too is a guarantee of freedom.

REFERENCES

Bell, D. (1977, June). Teletext and technology. *Encounter.* London; The social framework of the information society. In M. Dertouzos & J. Moses (Eds.), *The future of computers.* Cambridge, MA: MIT Press.

Bell, D. (1973). *The coming of post-industrial society.* New York: Basic Books.

Bell, D. (1977). The future world disorders: The structural context of crises. *Foreign Policy* (U.S.).

De Jouvenel, B. (1967). *The art of conjecture.* New York: Basic Books.

Goodman, D. (1978, December). Countdown to 1984. *The futurist.*

Minc, A. & Nora, S. (1978). La documentation francaise. *L'informatisation de la societe*, Harvard University program on information technology, 1976 & 1977.

Science, November 8, 1978.

7 Information for What Kind of Society?

HERBERT I. SCHILLER
University of California, San Diego

By and large, communication research in the United States is quixotic. Researchers intently study a world that does not really matter, whereas ignoring the one that does. Much of the work that is done "seems" to be dealing with reality. Communication research concerns itself, among other matters, with development, literacy, broadened participation, and new modes that may provide greater choices. There are also studies of electronic utopias and ecologically inspired colonies in space, utilizing telecommunication to explore personal realms and distant galaxies.

The implicit assumption that things will turn out well is always present. The road is the right one, and the direction taken is promising. Sometimes, in brief periods of doubt, it is admitted that there may be a detour or a few potholes up the road a bit.

The Information Society: Social and Ethical Issues—the title of a 1981 symposium—may be symptomatic of the general condition. The major concern of the symposium was expressed in an initial statement by the conference organizer: "A communications revolution, such as is taking place at the present time, will have a tremendous impact on our society and will create certain social and ethical problems" (Salvaggio, 1980).

The statement assumes that if we're not careful, new developments in telecommunications may have unintended and potentially harmful impacts and consequences in the future. It is useful, according to the symposium's organizer, to consider these possibilities as early as possible.

106

In general, such anticipatory thinking is unusual and deserves credit. But in this instance the focus on the future may create more problems than it solves because it does not take account of current reality but shifts attention away from it. The question to be considered is not what *may* happen if a new communication technology runs amok. The issue is much more stark and immediate. The question is: How do we check a communication technology that is already running amok and that has had this tendency to do so built into it from the outset? In short, how do we deal with telecommunication systems that have been conceived, designed, built, and installed with the primary objectives being the *maintenance* of economic privilege and advantage and the *prevention* of the kind of social change that would overturn and eliminate this privilege?

Developments in telecommunications since the Second World War, with few exceptions, have satisfied these negative objectives. Yet it is amazing how little this has been perceived by those whose task it is to chart and analyze such phenomena. The prime example, and the one most pertinent to this chapter, is the vast military outlay that has been made by the U.S. government over the last 45 years. Communication technologies have received a great and growing share of these expenditures.

The attention and favor extended to telecommunications (now institutionalized in an information industry) have not been due to chance. Still it is puzzling that the armaments boom, and its runoff on communication technology escape the attention and concern of researchers and workers whose area of interest is at the center of these developments. It is hardly a secret that the armaments output in America has reached staggering levels.[1] Nobel laureate Hannes Alfven suggests that "perhaps it is appropriate to give the *Bulletin [of the Atomic Scientists'* doomsday] clock a third hand which would show the seconds we have left in the count down" (Alfven, 1981, p. 5).

Despite this, each new administration, following the course of previous administrations, has discovered a giant gap in American military preparedness. The ante is being raised once again. In the five-year period from 1982 to 1985, more than $1 trillion dollars (1000 billion) will be poured into military expenditures—on top of past trillions. A good chunk of this astronomical outlay will go to the production of new telecommunication systems.

Simon Ramo, founder and currently director of TRW, one of the corporate recipients of the population's tax money for military electronics products, explains the impact of the planned military expenditures on the information and communication sector:

[1]Such widely different observers as E. P. Thompson, the distinguised English historian, and Reverend Billy Graham share anxiety over the level of military spending and the amount of stockpiled weapons.

Our military expenditures will probably increase as a percentage of the GNP over the next decade, and this could be extremely pertinent and beneficial to our leadership position in information technology, especially in computers and communications. This is because the right way for us to enhance our military strength in weapons systems is through superior communication, command, control and overall utilization of our weapons systems—functions that depend on superior information technology (Ramo, 1980, p. 283).

Unlike most communication researchers, Simon Ramo has the priorities in their proper order.

Actually, what Ramo is anticipating has been the practice throughout most of the past four decades. The entire electronics industry is an outcome of military subsidy and encouragement. The early computers and all their successors were developed and built with government funds. Illustrative, "the ILLIAC, the largest and most advanced computer of the day [1960s], was developed with funds from the Advanced Research Projects Agency of the Department of Defense" (Kolata, 1981, p. 268).

The first communication satellite system was a military effort. Most of the satellites in the sky today are providing military data. In January 1981, *Science* reported that

the Army soon expects to have 13,000 computers, the Navy, 33,000, and the Air Force, 40,000. The software bill for military computers last year came to more than $3 billion (Broad, 1981, p. 31).

So great is the Department of Defense's utilization of this huge arsenal of computers that it is compelled to finance the development of a standardized computer language (ADA) to overcome its present reliance on more than 1000 computer languages. But in this area as well, military influence has had a long history. "The Pentagon," *Science* reminds, "was the driving force behind the development of COBOL (Common Business-Oriented Language), which was introduced in 1959 and is today used extensively around the world" (Broad, 1981, p. 31).

Still the development of computer languages is but one debt the information age owes to its military parentage. Much more direct, though far less accessible than ADA or COBOL, is the dense U.S. electronic espionage network that encircles the world, not excluding national territory. This, too, is a creation made possible by the most sophisticated communication technologies.

The super-secret National Security Agency (NSA), for example, works largely with satellites, microwave stations, and computers. "Its mission includes cracking enemy codes, developing unbreakable ciphers for the United States and, most importantly, monitoring, translating

and analyzing worldwide communications among nations, selected
foreign citizens and some corporations" (Taubman, 1981a).

Australia is practically an NSA preserve. The country serves as a con-
tinental base, across the Pacific Ocean, for a full complement of NSA
electronic installations, to be directed against the Soviet Union and any
other perceived adversary. It is described by one Australian reporter
as a "Massive eavesdropping on Australian communications. . . . conducted by facilities dotted around Australia as part of a U.S. nuclear
war fighting machine that has been nurtured on Australian soil by [an]
inner circle" (Toohey, 1980). Desmond Ball, who documented the U.S.
electronic presence in Australia, inscribed his book "For a Sovereign
Australia" (Ball, 1980).

Australians are not alone in having their communication—personal,
private, and governmental—intercepted and monitored. The NSA per-
forms the same functions with abandon around the world including
inside the United States. An NSA intercept station outside London, for
example, checks all incoming and outgoing United Kingdom–European
communication traffic. The annual budget for the operation of this
global assemblage of modern communication technology is a secret.
According to the *New York Times*, "Intelligence officials estimated the
agency's budget to be more than $2 billion a year, larger than that of
the Central Intelligence Agency" (Taubman, 1981). What does this huge
sum buy? Nothing less than what many generously call the "information society."

According to a report of Charles Morgan (who used data supplied
elsewhere by Harrison Salisbury), in 1973 alone, "NSA retrieved a total
of 23,346,587 individual communications . . ." Morgan notes with
astonishment that this figure is "not the number of individual communications *intercepted*; it is the number of communications *retrieved*
for full study by the NSA" (Morgan, 1980).

By 1980 the existence of the National Reconnaissance Office had been
revealed. Still another supersecret military agency, its mission "is to
oversee the development and operation of spy satellites used to
photograph foreign territory and to monitor international communications" (Taubman, 1981b). Its budget exceeds $2 billion a year. Its satellites
in the 1960s and '70s were used "to photograph antiwar demonstra-
tions and urban riots" (Taubman, 1981).

The CIA deserves mention at this point. It is no wallflower in the
business of electronic surveillance. Though it is no longer fashionable
to bring up Watergate, it will be remembered that the crew of bunglers
recruited by the Nixon high-command came out of the agency.

In sum, great amounts of the activity, a good share of the content,
and the general thrust of what is now defined as the information age
represent military and intelligence connections.

Scholarly work in telecommunications puts these matters differently. In what has become a familiar argument, the duality and ambiguity of the new communication instrumentation is emphasized. The potential for constructive as well as destructive ends is insisted upon. For instance, Anthony Oettinger, director of Harvard's Program on Information Resources Policy, writes:

> Tensions will continue because of the close kinship among the technical means used for sometimes antithetical purposes—keeping peace or waging war, gathering intelligence or mapping agricultural and mineral resources—improving communications for trade or for military command and control (Oettinger, 1980, pp. 191–198).

But is the new instrumentation truly indifferent to the uses to which it is applied? Can it be utilized for social and peaceful goals as well as its current applications to war and war preparations?

Given the prevailing structure of global industrial and military power, it is difficult to believe that the communications revolution is not the outcome of deliberate and extensive efforts to maintain a worldwide system of economic advantage. New information technologies have been invented, developed, and introduced to support the business component of this system and to enable a globe-girdling military communication network to be prepared to be the ultimate enforcer. These are the objectives of those who were instrumental in the development of the telecommunications industry. These objectives account in large measure for its genesis.

As former Deputy Assistant Secretary for Human Rights and Social Affairs Sarah Goddard Power explained:

> Either we will design, produce, market and distribute the most advanced products and services spun off by the communications revolution and, in so doing, reinforce our economic as well as political, social, and cultural *advantage*—or we will increasingly find ourselves in the position of consumer and debtor to those who do. . . . The question of how the world adapts to the communications revolution has been steadily moving up the list of international concerns over the last decade, and it has now emerged as a major point of contention in East-West and North-South relationships (Power, 1980).

Maintaining and reinforcing our advantage are the explicit grounds that activate and accelerate the communication revolution. There is no ambiguity or dualism here. It is not a question of either-or, good technology use or bad technology use. It is solely a matter of developing and using the new communication technology for holding on to the economic benefits derived from a world system of power. For this reason, insistence on the potential and positive features of the current communication instrumentation is disingenuous at best.

To be sure, a part of the technology is used to produce consumer products, games, and entertainment. Many of these are actually applications seeking a use. Assorted privateers of enterprise naturally make the most of the opportunities created by this technology.

It is also undeniable that the commercial utilization of telecommunications will affect the employment in the private and public sectors. The character of work itself will change; living patterns will alter. House, home, and family arrangements will change. What will not be different—not if the corporate-military directorate has anything to say about it—are basic relationships of authority, ownership, and hierarchy of skills.

All the same, domestically and internationally, the evolving telecommunications industry is being hailed and promoted as efficient, problem solving, and liberating. The capability for enormously expanded generation and transmission of volumes of information, the technical feasibility of two-way communication, and the choice and diversity that new information technologies allegedly will provide, are publicized widely as realizable goals, affording hope to disadvantaged and excluded nations, classes, and people. These are not only unrealizable objectives. Under prevailing circumstances, their enunciation is misleading and deceptive. Other than for a few meritorious functions (libraries, medicine, etc.), and these require close scrutiny as well, significant socially beneficial utilization of the new technologies requires societal restructuring. The notion that humanistic social change can be introduced incrementally, via the new technology is unrealistic to the point of fantasy.

The social potential that *may* exist in some of the new instrumentation can be developed appreciably only in totally different social-cultural-economic contexts. Claims, therefore, that the two-sidedness of the instrumentation—its potential for good or evil—necessitates its immediate development in the hope that the socially desirable side may be encouraged are either uninformed by history or, more likely, too well informed by special interest.

In the meantime, the world (especially the part of the world administered by the United States) is being hooked into electronic circuitry that serves to keep things under control for the transnational corporate community of IBM–Chase-Manhattan–Citicorp–Exxon–ARCO–CBS–J. Walter Thompson, and their friends. Transnational data flows within and among these business giants have become indispensable to the maintenance of the world business system. Additional networks thicken the connections and extend the system's influence (Schiller, 1981). The stronger the electronic networks established, the less likely the possibility for national autonomy and independent decision making, and the more likely an intensified patrolling and controlling of the Third World majority.

Surveillance, monitoring, and marketing are the near-certain outcomes of the utilization of new communication technologies, domestically and globally. The American public, half of which does not bother to vote in national elections, hears the good news that electronic referendums are around the corner. Sitting at home, in front of a so-called domestic information utility, the happy citizen will be able to exercise innumerable inconsequential choices on an electronic console in the living room. This, we are told, constitutes the most advanced form of democracy.

Actually, business and marketing, law and order, and war are the main progenitors of telecommunications and the chief users of the advanced systems and processes. Yet all these developments could scarcely have reached their current psychotic levels without the assistance of still another vital component in the national communications system: the mass media. The media use many forms of telecommunications in the production of their services—news, entertainment, drama, music, film—and this is crucial, they interpret for all of us why we are supposed to need the new technologies. In a conflict-of-interest situation that boggles the mind, the print and electronic media, more often than not, are part of larger conglomerates in the new information industries. Yet in their capacity as information providers, they instruct their readers, viewers, or listeners why massive armaments are good for everyone, why the demands of the poor (people and nations) are not to be taken seriously, and why the United States must lead the world.

In providing these guidelines, they treat all of us daily to belligerent bulletins, some of which could be primary documentation—if we survive—for a future war crimes tribunal, hearing testimony about our media gatekeepers. An issue of the *Columbia Journalism Review*, for example, carried an excessively cautious article, which nonetheless detailed the fondness of the press for presenting nuclear war to its readers, listeners, and viewers as a feasible, controllable option (Kaplan, 1981). In this particular account, the responsibility for nuclear war mongering is shifted to the shoulders of reporters, who are described as enamored with the jargon of Pentagon briefers. This may have helped to get the article printed, but it will not do as an explanation of why lunatic reportage of this character is published. War, even nuclear war, has become an option, to be used to hold on to a transnational empire, many components of which are becoming unstuck.

All of this means that "the information age" is a misnomer. So too is "the telecommunications revolution." A few advanced industrial societies are striving to assure their privileges in a revolutionary world in which at least 3 billion people no longer are accepting quietly their long-standing conditions of exploitation and servility. Information systems have been developed to maintain—albeit in new ways—(Schiller, 1981) relationships that secure the advantages enjoyed by a small part of humanity and disadvantages that afflict the large majority.

Consequently, it is a mistake to believe that the changes required to overcome the global, national, and local disparities in human existence will be facilitated by developing telecommunications systems. In fact, the opposite result may be expected. Existing differentials and inequities will be deepened and extended with the new instrumentation and processes, despite their loudly proclaimed and widely publicized potential benefits. Only *after* sweeping change inside dozens of nations, in which ages-old social relationships are uprooted and overturned, can the possibility of using new communication technologies for human advantage begin to be considered. It can be taken for granted, also, that the technologies applied at such a time hardly will approximate those now in use and in operation.

How would communication researchers and information workers in general relate to this situation? Actually, their contribution could be a worthy one. It would require serious social and ethical consideration of the new communications technology. It would require, however, a totally different stance from what has come to be expected of communication research and the allied information worker community. Historically, communication as a field of endeavor has served the interests of the industrial marketing community, the psychological branch of the military, and the information arm of the governing bureaucracy, especially its international side. In effect, these are core elements in the U.S. domestic and global empire. Unquestioning allegiance to these power centers is tantamount to a denial of social and ethical responsibility.

Accordingly, to be socially responsible, communication workers, and theoretical and practical workers alike, must distance themselves as best they can from the centers of power. This is no simple or easy task. It means, first and foremost, to challenge the central sources of communication control and distortion in the country. It requires, for example, that the unprecedented arms buildup in the country be understood and then explained by communication people, wherever they have an opportunity to do so, as an effort to maintain the global status quo, as a way of denying resources and political autonomy to much of the world, and as the main source of the new electronic technologies, which are applied to governance, coercion, and control.

The social forces and institutional structures that produce the need for nuclear weapons are the proper subjects for research, analysis, and presentation. The connection of nuclear arsenals and plants of physical annihilation to the supportive informational system—the mass media—requires no less attention and debate.

In sum, what telecommunications as a field has as its domain of research, study, and subject matter for popular presentation, if it would accept its social responsibility, is nothing less than the physical, structural, and institutional bases for a system of domination that operates through its impact on human consciousness. No one could say that this is an easy assignment. The interlocking networks of power and authority that have grown up in this country in the 20th century make an adversary position disagreeable and difficult, and perhaps dangerous. Even the small space for an independent critique that once existed in the academic realm (and it was a small space, to be sure) is being recaptured by a rapidly forming corporate-university entente.

But the subject at hand is social and ethical responsibility. Is there any viable choice other than one of critical opposition to the foundations of what is now hailed as the "information society"?

REFERENCES

Alfven, H. (1981, January). Human IQ vs. nuclear IQ. *Bulletin of the Atomic Scientists*, p. 5.

Ball, D. (1980). *A suitable piece of real estate*. Sydney, Australia: Hale & Iremonger.

Broad, W. J. (1981). Pentagon orders end to computer babel. *Science, 211*, 31–33.

Kaplan, F. (1981, January/February). Going native without a field map. *Columbia Journalism Review*, 23–29.

Kolata, G. B. (1981, January). Who will build the next supercomputer? *Science, 211*, 268–269.

Morgan, C. (1980, December 17–24). The spies that hear all. *San Diego Newsline 4*, no. 11.

Oettinger, A. G. (1980, July 4). Information resources: Knowledge and power in the 21st century. *Science, 209*, 191–198.

Power, S. G. (1980). United States Department of State, Bureau of Public Affairs. *The communications revolution* (Current Policy No. 254). Washington, DC: Government Printing Office.

Salvaggio, J. L. (1980). *Statement of purpose*. Paper presented at the Edward R. Murrow Symposium.

Schiller, H. I. (1981). *Who knows: Information in the age of fortune 500*. Norwood, NJ: Ablex.

Taubman, P. (1981, February 2). Choice for C.I.A. deputy is an electronic-age spy. *New York Times*.

Toohey, B. (1980a, November 16–22). How Australians are kept in the dark (while the U.S. listens in). *National Times* (Australia).

8 Is Privacy Possible in an Information Society?

JERRY L. SALVAGGIO
Corpus Christi, Texas

As the transition from industrial to information societies unfolds, certain social characteristics are gradually being unveiled. The peaks and valleys of information societies are coming into clearer focus. One of the valleys may very well be that privacy is becoming as obsolete as the pachyderm, much like computers of the 1960s. Technicians have found manifold ways to use ever-shrinking memory chips, transmitters, and computer software to capture data on individuals which can now only be measured in gigabytes (billions of bytes) of information.

The idea that information technology is a natural threat to privacy is certainly not new. The anxieties of civil libertarians merely heightened when they realized that a whole new breed of computer and telecommunication systems had spawned vast databases and myriad electronic devices. Many scholars from various disciplines consider invasion of privacy to be the most serious problem we will be confronted with in an information society, because such a society is characterized by sophisticated forms of information technology which make it possible to gather and disseminate information instantaneously. Information is now collected in massive quantities, manipulated in innumerable ways, and shared with others in minutes, and all without the awareness of the subject of the information. Even a small database in a personal computer owned by the president of a coin club is capable of collecting and manipulating information in ways which government agencies could not even imagine in the 1940s.

PREVIOUS LITERATURE

Although most observers have viewed the computerization of society with awe, many have also considered the downside. Fifty years before the advent of the computer, Samuel Warren and Louis Brandeis (Warren & Brandeis, 1890) stressed the importance of privacy in society and the need for specific laws. A number of thoughtful, philosophical studies on privacy issues have been published in recent years (Cf., Reiman, 1976; Weiss, 1983). Schoeman's (1984) collection contains additional essays that probe the philosophical aspects of privacy. Privacy issues from a legal perspective have come into sharper focus in the past decade. Some of the more interesting pieces are found in law journals, especially the *Yale Law Review* and the *Rutgers Law Review*.

Research on how computers radically alter the way by which governments collect and abuse information on individuals is fairly well established, though far from complete. It has been argued that invasion of privacy is often a by-product of emphasizing law enforcement and national security. As criminal activity and military espionage increase, the need for greater surveillance increases (Marchand, 1980).

Donner (1981) claims that both government and private industry have a history of constructing files on citizens in the interest of national security. Bamford (1982) directs attention to the surveillance potential of the National Security Agency. Research on congressional policy relative to surveillance can be found in a variety of government reports (see Schwartz, 1985).

A recent government report (Electronic Surveillance and Civil Liberties, 1986) claims that electronic surveillance has become the epitome of the two-edged sword of technology for Americans. The report more than corroborated what scholars and civil libertarians had suspected for more than a decade—that invasion of privacy is one of the more serious problems associated with information societies.

In addition to scholarly studies, a number of general articles and publications on computer technology and privacy have explored the quiescent threat of privacy invasion in an information society (Brickenridge, 1970; Burnham, 1983, 1984, 1986; Earley, 1986; Linowes, 1978).

International comparisons of how privacy issues are handled by different countries are still scarce, but a few studies have been published (Mellors & Pollitt, 1984).

ASSESSING THE DAMAGE

The task of demonstrating that information technology is presently being used to invade the privacy of Americans is made relatively easy as examples abound in all walks of life. In what follows, I will describe various ways in which information technology is being used or abused depending on one's perspective. Whether these procedures constitute an invasion of privacy is a legal and/or moral question, which is not dealt with here.

Computer Databases

Mainframe computers have been a repository for dossiers on individuals in the United States since the mid-1950s. How many databases exist on the average individual in these systems would be difficult to calculate. In 1982, 16 government departments had a combined total of 3,529,743,665 files on American citizens. The numbers are much higher today and the files are assessable through more sophisticated database systems. The figures for law enforcement agencies are even higher. Approximately 288 million records on 114 million persons are stored on 85 computerized law enforcement systems (Who is watching you, 1982). Most of these systems are equipped with far more memory and speed than their predecessors. Moreover, the added capability of telecommunication links has led to heightened activity in the area of data collection.

The following organizations routinely collect data on individuals: hospitals, governmental agencies, law enforcement agencies, federal agencies dealing with organized crime and national security (immigration, Secret Service, Drug, etc.), credit agencies, employers, insurance companies, courts, banks, direct mail marketers, market research firms, car rental agencies, psychologists, lawyers, universities, schools, accountants, licensing boards, the armed services, cable companies, utilities, and many more. The types of information collected include: consumer, employment, educational, financial, medical, psychological, criminal, legal, and travel. How the ubiquitous collection and sharing of all this information affects individuals is not yet documented. What is known is that the number of files cascading from computers in a whirlwind of information-processing activity is resulting in a web of dossiers on virtually every member of information societies.

Intelligence agencies and law enforcement organizations hoard millions of files on American citizens for a number of reasons—most of which are no doubt valid. The Federal Bureau of Investigation (FBI), the Central Intelligence Agency (CIA), and the National Security Agency (NSA) have been targets of criticism for the potential they have for capturing data (Bamford, 1982; Burnham, 1984; Donner, 1981; Schiller, 1983). Although there is no evidence that these agencies have deliberately abused their snooping capabilities on a consistent basis, there is reason for concern given the sophisticated surveillance technologies at their disposal and previous transgressions by some of these agencies.

Potential Government Abuse

U.S. intelligence agencies receive an estimated $28 billion in annual funding (The House that Casey Built, 1987). The largest share goes to the Tactical Intelligence and Related Activities (TIARA) which collects $14 billion to manage warning satellites and reconnaissance aircraft. The CIA gets 10% of $3 billion. The NSA reportedly receives $4 billion.

The FBI has amassed a staggering number of documents on groups and individuals—the accuracy of which is now in doubt. A 1984 study found that the local arrest statistics which the FBI publishes each year are highly inaccurate (Burnham, 1984). Problems with the FBI's database, according to the study, stem from widespread violations of the established FBI rules and procedures.

Very little is known about how extensive the National Security Agency surveillance capabilities are. Schiller (1983) quotes a report that indicates that the NSA, in one year, retrieved for full study a total of 23,346,587 individual communications. He concludes that the NSA's budget of $2 billion a year has bought the information society. What is known is that the NSA is capable of monitoring thousands of telephone calls with an elaborate microwave system (Bamford, 1982). There is no evidence that the NSA routinely conducts surveillance of the typical American.

Law enforcement agencies have spied on several groups in the past. As a result of a 1984 lawsuit, it is now known that scores of police agencies worked together to spy on political, civic, and antiwar groups in the 1960s (Nationwide police spying in the 1960s is documented after court order, 1984). In the course of the trial, hundreds of police documents were made public and it was learned that the Chicago Police Department's "red squad" traded information with 159 agencies in 33 states. The agencies which participated in the spying ring included 100 municipal police departments, state law enforcement agencies, 16 county sheriff's offices, and 17 other public and private agencies.

The federal government has taken some precautions relative to privacy threats within its own agencies. Each executive department now has an office of the Inspector General (IG). Each IG conducts audits and investigates particular programs and operations to see that agencies are in compliance with current government rules pertaining to privacy. The *Federal Managers' Financial Integrity Act*, passed in 1982, requires that evaluations be conducted under specific standards and that there be a personal accountability for any false or misleading information given during evaluations. Whether these procedures are sufficient to control potential privacy abuses remains open to question.

New Technologies—New Techniques

Ellul (1963) argues that technology cannot be easily controlled—even by those with good intentions under the best of circumstances. He created the term *technological determinism* to describe the tendency for technology to create dependency thus further promoting its own uncontrolled evolution. The unprecedented appearance of technologies dealing with surveillance would seem to support Ellul's theory.

Space does not permit an exhaustive description of all the technologies available to government agencies, but the following table lists of those found by the Office of Technology.

COMPUTER MATCHING

More consequential than the growth of dossiers on individuals in government and private computers is the ability to store, manipulate, scan, trade, sell, and distribute information in a far more efficient and detailed manner. Compatible mainframes are capable of searching through each other's files in a technique called "computer matching." One computer is provided with a magnetic tape containing the records of another computer (e.g., a list of names). With computer matching, the IRS can match tax returns with files provided by country clubs and exclusive car dealers assuming the latter are willing to sell the IRS their computer tapes. Thus far, the IRS has not had much success.

Advances in network software does not augur well for securing the data in these files. Prior to the 1980s, mainframe and microcomputers were limited in the ways they could communicate with each other. IBM's System Network Architecture (SNA) software improved this considerably, and the new generation of IBM personal computers will improve micro to mainframe communication to an unprecedented degree. The Office of Technology Assessment Report (1985) notes: "It is technically feasible to have an interconnected electronic network of Federal criminal justice, other civilian, and perhaps even military record systems that would monitor many individual transactions with the Deferral Government and be the equivalent of a national database surveillance system."

A number of federal agencies have sought permission to use computer matching to detect fraud, locate draft dodgers, and monitor criminal activity. The IRS attempted to use life-style data to identify in-

TABLE 8.1 Electronic Surveillance Technology:
Current and Planned Agency Use

Technology	Number of agency components reporting		
	Current	Planned	Total
Closed Circuit	25	4	29
Night vision systems	21	1	22
Miniature transmitters	19	2	21
Radio receivers (scanners)	19	1	20
Vehicle beepers	13	2	15
Sensors	12	3	15
Telephone taps	13	1	14
Pen registers	11	1	14
Telephone usage monitoring	7	3	10
Computer usage monitoring	4	2	6
Electronic mail monitoring	1	5	6
Cellular radio interception	3	2	5
Pattern recognition systems	2	2	4
Satellite interception	1	3	4
Expert systems/AI	0	3	3
Voice recognition	0	3	3
Satellite-based surveillance	1	1	2
Fiber optic interception	0	1	1

Source: Office of Technical Assessment, 1985

dividuals who may have underreported their income tax. Sources of information for the IRS study included telephone books, automobile registration files, and statistical information about the average income of the families compiled by the Census Bureau.

That some government departments have come dangerously close to exploiting their computer matching technology is well documented and is being studied by various Congressional committees. *Computer Matching and Privacy Protection Act of 1986* (S 2756), a bill proposed by Bill Cohen (R-Maine), attests to the seriousness of the problem.

Interactive Computer Systems

The databases previously discussed have one commonality—the collection of information occurs when applications and other forms are completed. In interactive cable TV and in videotex systems, the computer scans homes every few seconds collecting data automatically. Information gathered through interactive cable generally includes movies viewed, home shopping, opinion polls, and security. The mainframe computer, at the head end of the cable company, tabulates returning signals to ascertain if a TV set is on, if a pay movie is being watched, or if a burglar alarm has been tripped. Most of this data is then used for billing, not for building dossiers. In order to use the system as a dossier, a cable operator must write a specific program requesting the computer to output all information on a particular individual over a given period of time. Because most interactive cable systems do not have such programs, retrieving this information involves a considerable expense and the efforts of a computer program.

Yet, the information that can be extracted from a cable system is considerable. Signals returning to the computer reveal programs watched, products purchased through teleshopping, and hours and minutes the family viewed each channel. All of this can be matched with zip codes and correlated with income. Although the *Cable Communications Act of 1984* prohibits the sale of this information without permission, it can be subpoenaed by law enforcement agencies and accessed by cable employees.

Videotex systems are an even greater quiescent peril to privacy than two-way cable systems because they store complete conversations and record the names of every article accessed by the subscriber. Each request for newspaper and magazine articles, government publications, airline schedules, encyclopedia articles, company profiles, and bulletin boards is recorded and stored. User groups carry on extensive conversations, often sharing intimate information.

However, it should be pointed out that although the potential is there, videotex operators have little to gain by accessing and/or saving individual communications.

Employee Monitoring

In the systems reviewed above, the participants are generally cognizant of the fact that information about them is being collected. Other forms of monitoring are more furtive. Employers are increasingly gathering information on subordinates in order to learn more about their potential behavior patterns. A number of corporations are using computer programs to classify possible drug abusers. Joseph H. Lodge, president of Corporate Security Advisors in Miami, has boasted: "We can look at information in personnel files and rate or rank each employee according to their drug use" (Faber, 1983, p. 1). If this technique is perceived as an effective means of evaluating potential problem employees, it is likely to become commonplace. The problem is that the technique is based on the assumption that social psychology is a science. False conclusions can be drawn as a result of poorly trained personnel or as a result of prescribed medication.

The polygraph, though highly controversial, continues to be viewed as a scientific instrument capable of dividing the good from the bad. As the polygraph is used today, employees and prospective employees have little choice but to submit to an exam that involves answering intimate questions having little to do with the nature of the employment. Approximately 2,000,000 individuals a year reportedly undergo polygraph tests. Brokerage firms, banks, retail stores, and government agencies routinely use the polygraph.

The accuracy of the polygraph is still being debated though the OTA has reported that the scientific validity of the polygraph cannot be established. If experts are correct, and the tests are only 90% accurate, it is estimated that 10% or 50,000 individuals are deprived of employment unfairly (Who Is Watching You, 1982).

The House of Representatives recently rejected (241 to 173) a move to authorize the widespread use of polygraphs in private industry. The House also has a bill that would ban most private companies from giving polygraph tests to prospective or current employees.

Bell Laboratories, ABC, the Wharton School, and the Institute for Social Management in Bulgaria are among those institutions reported to be using a new computer technique referred to as *block modeling*. Block modeling uses innocuous information such as—Whom you talk with in your company; whose phone calls you do not return; who you eat lunch with; whom you have worked with, etc. Microcomputers are used to identify patterns of working relationships. As Boorman and Leavitt (1983) wrote, "There are discrete sets of people occupying similar positions in the relationship networks, and who are thus likely to behave similarly in ways important to the organization, and can be candidates for receiving similar treatment." The authors further observe:

> . . . these methods have the capacity to capitalize on the unguarded moments of ordinary people; to probe organizations for factional alignments in a low-visibility and therefore insidious way; to play to human biases—particularly among managers—to name names; and to give sometimes facile technological rationales for settling complex personnel problems. (p. 3)

VISUAL SURVEILLANCE

Techniques that use infrared photography, closed circuit TV, satellite, and night image intensifiers are referred to as visual surveillance via optical/imaging. The cost of video cameras has come down dramatically in recent years making them available to even small shops. Newer models are designed to operate through peep holes and are capable of zooming in on individuals. Closed circuit video cameras, some with infrared capabilities, are routinely used by many organizations to monitor parking lots, elevators, hallways, bank lobbies, and cash registers. Almost all banks, retail stores, and restaurants are equipped with cameras and tape recorders. Ostensibly the video camera is there to provide a description of suspects after an organization is robbed. In interviews, most employees of fast-food retail stores, both in the United States and Japan, have admitted that the tapes are viewed each week by the store manager to identify employee problems. New recorders make it possible to scan through hours of video tape in minutes.

Data Surveillance

Data surveillance is a relatively novel technique that has become afford-able to large corporations. Employers assigned to the job of data input generally work on dumb terminals (no local memory or CPU) tied into mainframes. Mainframe software is capable of recording the total number of minutes per day an employee worked and the number of key strokes each terminal operator typed. The program tells an employer how many times a particular word processor was inactive, thus in-dicating how often the employee took breaks and the average length of each break. Several firms base salaries, promotions, and bonuses on these reports (The Boss That Never Blinks, 1986).

Telephone use by employees is routinely monitored by checking the public branch exchange (PBX). PBXs are telephone computer switching systems, usually located on the premises, that route telephone calls and incoming computer data to the proper telephone or terminal in the building. The most recent generation of PBXs are not only capable of monitoring all out-going calls but provide computer printouts each month of all calls made by employees. A cross-check of the employee's personal records indicates how often the employee is calling home or to a spouse or making unauthorized long-distance phone calls. Few organizations inform employees of this procedure.

SENSOR TECHNOLOGY

Sensor technology includes magnetic, seismic, infrared, and elec-tromagnetic sensors that can be placed on vehicles, buried in the ground or implanted on a person. Most sensor devices are used to track move-ment of individuals. Executives and politicians can be equipped with sensor devices that can be triggered in case of a kidnapping.

The highway department in Hong Kong is using an electronic sensor for a new road pricing plan. Vehicles are fitted with an electronic number plate which is placed under the chassis. When the vehicle passes certain points in Hong Kong where sensors are placed, a signal is sent to an electronic loop buried underground. The computer correlates the number with the owner of the vehicle, tabulates the number of times the vehicle has passed the point and bills the owner for a road tax. Although the system is designed as a means to tax those who use the roads, the potential for tracking individual movement is inherent in the system.

More ominous is the use of sensor technologies on humans. Electronic tracking devices similar to those used to tag wild animals are now being tested on parolees. According to Robert Weigle, who proposed a penal institution plan, an ankle bracelet could be attached to those early parolees. Weigle observes that the concept could be taken one step further and a device implanted in the brain that could monitor the parts of the mind that produce negative or violent responses. Although implanted sensors seem radical today, their use is almost certain to grow exponentially in the years ahead. Implanted sensors are a logical answer to lost children and potential victims of kidnappers.

LEGAL PROTECTION

Optimists generally dismiss the invasion of privacy as a serious social problem. Most argue that legislation will provide a safeguard when and if invasion of privacy becomes a problem. A quick historical examination of privacy laws disputes this contention. An amalgam of torts and principles found in the Constitution guarantee individuals in the United States that privacy is a right. Tort law is designed to prohibit government or individuals from subjecting individuals to tensions by revealing humiliating and annoying invasion of an individual's solitude. The First, Fourth and Fifth amendments are generally cited as the sources of most Constitutional protection.

The U.S. *Privacy Act of 1974* was designed to protect individuals from unauthorized access to government data pertaining to themselves. Government agencies, under this law, are prohibited from disclosing personal information except under court order. The law, however, was vague and made obsolete by the technology that evolved since the late 1970s. A current government publication suggests that "new applications of personal information have undermined the goal of the Privacy Act . . ." (Electronic Surveillance and Civil Liberties, 1986).

More recently, stronger bills have been written. In June, 1986, the House of Representatives passed a landmark legislation that extends federal protection to electronic communications from invasion or interference. *The Electronic Communications Privacy Act of 1986* covers electronic mail, paging devices, cordless and cellular phones, and digital networks. The bill is aimed not only at government itself but at hackers. Government interception of electronic communications, under this bill, will require court ordered warrants.

There is little doubt that more legislation will be put forward and will provide stiffer penalties for anyone caught violating the rules. However, it would be naive to assume that laws will protect individuals from those who find reason to seek out information on their personal lives. Laws have provided little protection from invasion of privacy thus far.

As an example, simultaneous with the submission of the above bill, the Reagan administration is seeking to computerize government records to reduce fraud in federal welfare programs. In essence, the Office of Management and Budget (OMB) is requiring income verification programs that will require states to tap into bank records, private credit-checking agencies, or hospital records if it is legal in that state (Earley, 1986). The OMB points out that it is not setting up one single national computer system but rather 54 state-territorial systems operating independently from each other. Although this is true, it is already clear that the OMB requirements imposed on the participating states amounts to one computer system centrally operated from Washington, D.C.

As previously discussed, sharing computer data among different government agencies without the permission of the individual is prohibited by the Privacy Act of 1974. When the Department of Health, Education and Welfare (HEW), under Joseph A. Califano, Jr., sought to put Project Match into operation, it was pointed out to HEW that matching was illegal. HEW attorneys then suggested, in a 12-page memo, that the Privacy Act restrictions could be circumvented if HEW treated the record exchange as something other than a disclosure of records. It was suggested that HEW describe its record request as interdepartmental assistance.

This illustration demonstrates that laws do not provide a safeguard against invasion of privacy. Laws are open to interpretation and exclude certain agencies. Moreover, those who violate these laws are difficult to catch and difficult to prosecute.

I have described various technologies and have attempted to demonstrate that laws are not adequate protection against abuse of information technology. The question that remains is whether organizations will use these technologies to intrude on the privacy of employees and the public, if it is clear that they represent an invasion of privacy. This depends on organizational behavior. Organizations, like individuals, vary in their willingness to violate codes of ethics and laws. The issues

are even more complicated considering the degree to which ethical violations can be justified. Offered below are three fictitious cases representing various situations that organizations are faced with every day.

Case 1

A manager of a large department store is informed that her department
lost more than $30,000 last year due to shoplifting. Two new measures
are recommended. First, the manager should order all employees to
take a polygraph. Secondly, the manager should install two-way mir-
rors equipped with hidden video cameras in all the dressing rooms.

Case 2

An operations manager of a large firm is informed by the vice president for financial affairs that the long distance telephone bills have risen
dramatically over the past year, indicating possible employee abuse.
The operations manager apprises his superior that the new PBX recently
installed can produce a monthly readout of all numbers called by an
employee and can further correlate the numbers called with local
establishments and the numbers of spouses. The vice president exhorts
the operations manager to activate this feature as soon as possible.

Case 3

A major insurance firm, which routinely invests several hundreds of
thousands of dollars into employees with managerial potential, is considering a block modeling program. The program will use data collected
surreptitiously and then correlate the information with psychological
profiles that supposedly identify managerial potential. Information collected will include employee habits (coffee breaks, telephone usage),
personal networking (other employees he or she associates with) and
personal life style (dress, car, etc.).

The above cases have several things in common. Each entails ques-
tionable utilization of information technology and all are currently being used in the United States, though most are not yet commonplace.
Also, in each case the utilization of information technology is a cost
savings for the organization.

Individuals within an organization may recognize the infringement
on individual privacy. If so, he or she is confronted with a difficult question: "Is this in the *organization's best interest?*" This question was probably asked by IRS officials before deciding to purchase personal life-

style data on individuals to be cross-checked with income tax returns. The question was apparently answered in the affirmative.

A related series of questions might hypothetically be asked. Is the intrusion of privacy in the best interest of the decision-maker, and is it in the best interest of the public? Because what is good for the organization is likely to be good for the individual, this question is generally answered affirmatively. In addition to these two questions, the decision maker might ask, "Is this in the public's best interest?" When the answer to this question is in conflict with the answer to the first two questions, a fourth question might be asked. "Do the interests of the organization outweigh the interests of the public?"

The problem with the above question and answer series is that the probe is deceptively simple. In Case 1, for example, the extra surveillance is clearly in the organization's best interest and in the best interest of the manager. Although the technique would seem to be an intrusion of the privacy of customers, and therefore not in the best interest of the public, the manager could counter that if the act results in less loss of product due to shoplifting, the cost savings passed on to the customer would justify the loss of privacy.

In Case 1 the rationale of the department store is to minimize losses. That the act is a threat to the privacy of the store's customers is considered a small price to pay if incidents of theft can be reduced. If this is the outcome, then the department store can argue that telecommunications was not only in the best interest of the department store (organization) but also in the best interest of the public because the cost savings will be passed on to the public.

In Case 2 the monitoring of the PBX can be rationalized on the basis of minimizing losses and maximizing profits for shareholders.

Even block modeling as seen in Case 3 can be rationalized despite its violation of privacy. Identification of individuals with managerial potential benefits the firm and the employees. Furthermore, problematic employees might be identified at an early stage. That the technique might result in the loss of excellent employees due to a weakness in the program is a small price to pay for selective grooming.

Intrusions on one's privacy, no matter how insidious, are almost always within the realm of justification. In reference to use of implanted body sensors used to monitor parolee whereabouts, one scholar (Fried, 1984) observes:

> Although monitoring is admitted to be unusually intrusive, it is argued that this particular use of monitoring is entirely proper, since it justifies the release of the persons who would otherwise remain in prison, and since surely there is little that is more intrusive and unprivate than a prison regime. (p. 206)

When privacy issues are totally dissected as in these three cases, they are generally reducible to loss of privacy versus loss of profits. Days Inns of America, a national motel chain, testified to Congress that it cut losses from employee crime from $1 million in 1975 to $115,000 in 1984 through polygraphs. One would be hard put to convince the management of Days Inns that the polygraph is not 100% foolproof in light the practical results they have experienced.

Privacy problems are generally rationalized on the basis of organizational interest and public interest. David Linowes (1978) put it this way: "The computer is not the problem. The problem is balancing a citizen's privacy rights with the quest for government efficiency." Linowes could have inserted corporate efficiency as well. Because increased use of information technology for surveillance is so easily rationalized on the basis of economics, efficiency, and security, the threat of information technology to privacy is increased. Individuals in decision-making situations, it is argued here, are pressured to invade the privacy of others. Decision makers are willing to do so because the act can be rationalized on the basis of being in the organization's and the public's best interest. Corporate loyalty will generally outweigh public interest.

DISCUSSION

Invasion of privacy is perhaps the most serious problem associated with information societies (Westin, 1967). This dire conclusion is based on the fact that invasion of privacy is a social problem that will be extremely difficult to solve. Newer, more powerful and more sophisticated forms of technology are revealed every week and, as crime escalates, surveillance increases. The 8-bit microprocessor has been replaced by the 16-bit, which is now being replaced by the 32-bit machine. The 1-megabit chip announced in 1985 is being replaced with the 4-megabit chip, which will soon be replaced with the 16-megabit chip announced by the Japanese in 1987. The new generation of microcomputers are inexpensive and more powerful than $300,000 mainframe computers sold in the late 1970s. As a result, mid-level government official and corporate employees now have capabilities that previously required cabinet and executive level approval.

Laws seem inadequate when dealing with the vagaries of information. The time span between identification of a privacy problem and passage of a new law is a minimum of several years.

Many individuals do not place a high value on privacy. When a new video camera is placed in an organization, employees may become angry, but most are not in a position to demand its removal. Within weeks, the camera has become part of the store's facilities and is forgotten.

The most serious set back for maintaining privacy in an information society is not the growth of technology or the difficulty of passing legislation, but the fact that invasion of privacy is so easily rationalized. As we have seen, privacy is often sacrificed for more valued commodities—profits, efficiency, and productivity. When two concepts cannot coexist, the one that is most valued survives.

REFERENCES

Bamford, J. (1982). *The puzzle palace.* Boston: Houghton Mifflin.

Boorman, S. A., & Leavitt, P. R. (1983, Nov. 20). Big brother and block modeling. *The New York Times,* p. 3

The boss that never blinks. (1986, July 28) *Time,* pp. 46–47.

Breckenridge, A. C. (1970). *The right to privacy.* Lincoln: University of Nebraska Press.

A Buck Rogers' type of concept: Electronic parolee surveillance, brain for criminals suggested. (1982, October 26). *The Houston Post,* p. 11A. 1982.

Burnham, D. (1983, October 27). Computer fraud in 12 U.S. agencies put far above 172 cases. *The New York Times,* p. 4.

Burnham, D. (1984, July 29) F.B.I. arrest data found inaccurate *The New York Times,* p. 14.

Burnham, D. (1986, January 19). Computer data faulted in suit over wrongful arrest. *The New York Times.*

Donner, F. (1981) *The age of surveillance: the aims and methods of America's political intelligence system.* New York: Vintage.

Earley, P. (1986, May 18) Big brother alive and well in U.S. maze of computers. *Washington Post,* reprinted in *Houston Chronicle,* p. 22.

Ellul, J. (1964). *The technological society.* New York: Alfred A. Knopf.

Electronic Surveillance and Civil Liberties, Washington DC: (1986) Office of Technology Assessment.

Fried, C. (1984). Privacy. In Schoeman, F. D. (Ed.), *Philosophical Dimensions of Privacy: An Anthology,* (pp. 203–222). New York: Cambridge University Press.

Faber, 1983: 1)

The House that Casey Built. (1987, February 15). AP press release, printed in *The Mexico City News,* p. 6.

Linowes, D. F. (1978, June 26). The privacy crisis. *Newsweek,* p. 19.

Marchand, D. G. (1980). *The politics of privacy, computers, and criminal justice records.* Arlington, VA: Information Resources Press.

Mellors, C., & Pollitt, D. (1984). Legislating for privacy: data protection in Western Europe. *Parliamentary Affairs,* 199–215.

Nationwide police spying in 60s is documented after court order, (1984, Dec. 6) *The New York Times,* p. 13.

Personal privacy in an Information Society, (The Report of the Privacy Protection Study Commission). (1977). Washington, DC: U.S. Government Printing Office.

Reiman, J. (1976). Why privacy is important, *Philosophy and Public Affairs,* pp. 22–44.

Schiller, H. (1983). In Jerry L. Salvaggio, (Ed.) *Telecommunications: Issues and choices for society,* (pp. 24–33). New York: Longman.

Schoeman, F. D. (1984). *Philosophical dimensions of privacy: An anthology.* London: Cambridge University Press.

Warren, S., & Brandeis, L. (1890). The right to privacy. *Harvard Law Review,* 193–220.

Weiss, L. B. (1983, Feb. 26). Government steps up use of computer matching to find fraud in programs. *Congressional Quarterly Weekly Report,* 432.

Westin, A. F., & Baker, M. A. (1972). *Databanks in a free society: Computers, record-keeping and privacy.* New York: Quadrangle.

Who Is watching you. (1982). *U.S. News and World Report.* p. 32.

Selected Reading

Anderson, H. M., & Yerkes, R. M. (1915). The importance of social status indicated by the results of the pointscale method of measuring mental capacity. *Journal of Educational Psychology, 6.* 137–150.

Arendt, H. (1985). *The Human Condition.* Chicago: University of Chicago Press.

Atwater, T. Brown, Brown, N., & Heeter, C. (1986, May). *Foreshadowing the electronic publishing age: First exposures to viewtron.* Paper presented at the International Communication Association Annual Convention, Chicago, IL.

Atwater, T., & Brown, N. A. (1985, November). *Videotex news: A content analysis of three videotex services and their companion newspapers.* Paper presented at the meeting of Speech Communication Association Annual Convention, Denver, CO.

Appleton, H., Conner, R. F., Cook, T. D., Schaffer, D., Tamkin, G., & Weber, S. J. (1975). *Sesame street revisited.* New York: Russell Sage Foundation.

Bachrach, P., & Barataz, M. S. (1970). *Power and poverty.* New York: Oxford University Press.

Ball, D. (1980). *A suitable piece of real estate.* Sydney, Australia: Hale & Iremonger.

Blackhall, K. (1979). *Affordable privacy.* Telecommunications International Edition, 10, 96–104.

Blake, F. M. (1978). Public access to information in the post-industrial society. In E. J. Josey (Ed.), *The information society: Issues and answers.* Phoenix, AZ: Oryx Press.

Block, R. S. (1984). A global information utility. *The Futurist, 18,* 31–34.

Blumler, J. G., Dutton, W. H., & Kraemer, K. L. (Eds.) (1987). *Wired cities: Shaping the future of communications.* White Plains, NY: Knowledge Industries.

Bradley, H. G., Dordick, H. S., & Nanus, B. (1980). *The emerging network marketplace.* Norwood, NJ: Ablex.

Brock, G. W. (1981) *The telecommunications industry: The dynamics of market structure.* Cambridge, MA: Harvard University Press.

Carey, J. (1969). The communication revolution and the professional communicator. *Sociological Review Monograph, 13,* 23–28, 32.

Carey, J., & Quirk, J. J. (1970). The myths of the electronic revolution. *American Scholar, 39,* 219–241, 395–424.

Cheah, C., & Jussawalla, M. (1983). Toward an information economy: The case of Singapore. *Information Economics and Policy, 1*(2), 161–176.

Chen, M. (1986). *Social equity and computers in education.* Paper presented at the International Communication Association Annual Convention, Chicago, IL.

Cherns, A. (1980). Work and values: Shifting patterns in industrial society. *International Social Science Journal, 32*(3), 427–441.

Christians, C. G., & Hammond, L. (1986). Social justice and a community information utility. *Communication, 9,* 127–149.

Cleveland, H. (1984, November-December). King Canute and the information resource. *Computers and People,* 16–20. Center for Urban Affairs and Policy Research.

Computers and Community Organizations. Evanston, IL: Center for Urban Affairs and Policy Research, Northwestern University.

Crane, H. (1980). *The new social marketplace.* Norwood, NJ: Ablex.

Dervin, B. (1980). Communication gaps and inequities: Moving toward a reconceptualization. In B. Dervin & M. J. Voigt (Eds.), *Progress in Communication Sciences, Vol. II.* Norwood, NJ: Ablex.

Dervin, B. (1982). Citizen access as an information equity issue. In F. Gutierrez, J. R. Schement, & M. A. Sirbu (Eds.), *Telecommunication policy handbook.* New York: Praeger.

Donohue, G. A., Olien, C. N., & Tichenor, P. A. (1970). Mass media and differential growth of knowledge. *Public Opinion Quarterly, 34,* 158–170.

Dordick, H. S., Lievrouw, L. A., & Schement, J. R. (1983). The information society in California: Social factors influencing its emergence. *Telecommunications Policy, 7*(1), 64–72.

Dozier, D. M., & Rice, R. E. (1984). Rival theories of electronic newsreading. In R. E. Rice (Ed.), *The new media: Communication, research and technology.* Beverly Hills, CA: Sage.

Ducker, J. (1984). Multiplying databases around the world. *Intermedia, 12,* 82–83.

Ettema, J. S. (1984). Three phases in the creation of information inequities: An empirical assessment of a prototype videotex system. *Journal of Broadcasting, 28,* 383–395.

Farrell, T. B., & Goodnight, G. T. (1981). Accidental rhetoric: The root metaphors of three mile island. *Communication Monographs, 48,* 271–330, 273.

Garnham, N. (1986). The media and the public sphere. *Intermedia, 14,* 28–33.

Gill, C., & Larsen, J. K. (1984). *Changing lifestyles in Silicon Valley.* Los Altos, CA: Cognos Associates.

Goldberg, L. (1986, March 10). L. A. videotex outlet not profitable enough. *Electronic Media, 26,* 48.

Goldberg, L. (1986, March 24). Videotex fortunes: Knightrider folds viewtron service. *Electronic Media, 24,* 3, 53.

Helleiner, G. K., & O'Brien, R. C., (1980). The political economy of information in a changing international economic order. *International Organization, 34*(4), 47.

Ito, Y. (1985). Implications of the Telecommunications Policy Reform in Japan. *Keio Communication Review, 6,* March, pp. 7–18.

Johnson, J. (1984). Videotex hits the office. *Datamations, 30,* 44–48.

Kochen, M. (1975). Evolution of brainlike social organs. *Information for action.* New York: Academic Press.

Larsen, J. K., & Rogers, E. M. (1984). *Silicon Valley fever.* New York: Basic Books.

Leed, E. (1980). 'Voice' and 'print': Master symbols in the history of communication. In K. Woodward (Ed.), *The myths of information: Technology and post-industrial culture.* Madison, WI: Coda Press.

Lerner, D. (1958). *The passing of traditional society.* Glencoe, IL: Free Press.

Logue, T. J. (1979). Teletext: Towards an information utility? *Journal of Communication, 29,* 58–65.

Mayo, J. S. (1985). The evolution of information technologies. *Information technologies and social transformation*. Washington, DC: National Academy Press.

McCorduck, P. (1979). *Machines who think*. San Francisco: W. H. Freeman.

McFarlan, W. F. (1984). Information technology changes the way you compete. *Harvard Business Review, 62*, 98–103.

Miller, T. (1983, September). Information, please, and fast. *Washington Journalism Review*, 51–53.

Miller, V. E., & Porter, M. E. (1985). How information gives you competitive advantage. *Harvard Business Review, 63*, 149–160.

Minc, A., & Simon, N. (1980). *Computerization and society*. Boston: MIT Press.

Neal, W. C. (1984). Technology as social progress: A commentary on knowledge and human capital. *Journal of Economic Issues, 18*, 573–580.

Nie, N., & Sackman, H. (Eds.) (1970). *The information utility and social choice*. Montvale, NJ: AFIPS Press.

Noble, D. (1984). The underside of computer literacy. *Raritan: A quarterly Review, 3*, 37–64, 52, 62.

Overduin, H. (1986). News judgment and the community, connection in the technological limbo of videotex. *Communication, 9*, 229–246.

Park, R. (1940). News as a form of knowledge: A chapter in the sociology of knowledge. *American Journal of Sociology, 45*, 669–686, 676.

Pelton, J. (1981). *Global talk*. Alpen aan den Rijn, Netherlands: Sijthoff & Noordhoff.

Roland, G. (1987). The post-1981 national policy context for new communication technologies. In Blumler, J. G., Dutton, W. H., & Kraemer, K. L. (Eds.), *Wired cities: Shaping the future of communications*. White Plains, NY: Knowledge Industries.

Rorty, R. (1983). Method and morality. *Social science as moral inquiry*. New York: Columbia University Press.

Ruben (Ed.), *Information and behavior (Vol. 1)*. New Brunswick, NJ: Transaction.

Ruchinkas, J. (1980). *The consumer in the electronic marketplace: How people use entertainment and information services*. (Report #7902). Los Angeles: University of Southern California Center for Communications Policy Research.

Salvaggio, J. L. (Ed.) *Telecommunications: Issues and choices for society*, New York: Longman, 1983.

Schiller, D. (1982) *Telematics and Government*. Norwood, NJ: Ablex.

Schudson, M. (1982). The politics of narrative form: The emergency of news conventions in print and television. *Daedalus, 111*, 97–112, 98.

Seick, S. K. (1984). Business-information systems and databases. *Annual Review of Information Science and Technology, Vol. 19*. White Plains, NY: Knowledge Industry Publications.

Sennett, R. (1974). *The fall of public man: On the social psychology of capitalism*. New York: Vintage.

Sieghart, P. (1981). The international implications of the development of Microelectronics. *The Information Society, 1*(1), 1–15.

Slack, J. D. (1984). *Communication technologies and society: Conceptions of causality and the politics of technological intervention*. Norwood, NJ: Ablex.

Smith, A. (1980). *Goodbye Gutenberg*. New York: Oxford University Press.

Toffler, A. (1970). *Future shock*. New York: Random House.

Weaver, D. A. (1983). *Videotex journalism: Teletext, viewdata and the news*. Hillsdale, NJ: Lawrence Erlbaum Associates.

Why the French are in love with videotex. (1986, January). *Business Week, 20*, 84–85.

Author Index

Subject Index